Foreword

Forget about Ptolemy; forget about Galileo. Your *head* is the centre of the universe. The sun and sky, the moon and the stars, the people and objects that make up your world, all revolve around your head. Indeed, the world you live in is created by your head – by the myriad nerve cells in your brain.

Of course, the impressions we have of the outside world are, to a large extent, interpretations of messages that the world sends us. Light, sounds and smells act as predictions about the things around us. Our sense organs convert energy and chemicals into electrical impulses – the currency of the brain – which tell us of objects beyond our reach. But perception is far more than a passive process, far more than a multi-media movie of the world playing inside our heads. Our brains *infer* the nature of the things around us, based largely on our personal knowledge, inherited and learned, of the way in which our world works.

The head is the triumph of animal evolution. Even the most primitive worm has a head – a brave protuberance, bristling with sense organs – which it thrusts forward into unknown territory. In human beings the head has reached its zenith. Almost too big for the birth canal; consuming one fifth of the oxygen and glucose in the circulating blood; carrying the face that proclaims our identity; requiring systems of movement and balance more sophisticated than any other part of the body.

The head is the beacon of a person, the repository of intelligence, the home of the mind.

Colin Blakemore
Wayneflete Professor of Physiology, University of Oxford
Chief Executive of The European Dana Alliance for the Brain

The art and science of what goes on in our heads

Central to the sciences of life is reading purposes and functions, from every scale of observable structures. Major insights of the past, were seeing bones of the skeleton as levers obeying principles of mechanics; seeing the crystalline in the eye as a lens obeying laws of optics; the heart as a pump; nerves as channels conveying coded information. These were more than analogies: they explained functions of the body, in terms of hands-on technologies and concepts of the physical sciences. So life itself was seen as energy controlled by information in structures of matter.

Would this emphasis on forms and structures, made alive with controlled energy, work for explaining mind in brain? For centuries the key structures for mind seemed to be holes in the brain – the ventricles. These were physical spaces, where mind might seem to live. It was an astonishing leap of imagination to think of structures of the brain creating thoughts and feelings of mind. Yet in the year of Newton's birth, Pascal showed that meshed gear wheels could do mental arithmetic.

Charles Babbage went further in the 1830's to design the first programmable computer, made of brass gears and steel pinions, to work through mathematical functions without need of human control or understanding of how it worked. It could only be understood by knowing abstract mathematical principles, on which it operated, as well as mechanical principles of its enmeshed gears. Was this the essence of brain-mind dualism seen in a machine? There are no gears in the head, but what of neurons? How do they function?

For millennia, it was current technologies that suggested how minds might work – strings, hydraulics, telephone exchanges – but now we see an opposite trend, feeding back into technology. For now we look to concepts of mind for designing intelligent machines.

It is remarkable that, for the price of a meal, we can buy a box of clever tricks that will beat its owner at the most intellectual game - Chess. For a similar price, we can buy a box filled with the silicon of sand that will recognize speech, and translate languages. Only a few years ago these would have been miracles; now we take them for granted. Yet although we think of the brain as a machine, we do not know how to reverse-engineer the brain, to build machines that feel pleasure and pain and appreciate art. The machine that recognizes and translates our words, does not *understand* them. My laptop checks my grammar, but with no understanding of what I am trying to convey. We may look for the basis of consciousness in engineering principles of the nervous system, yet no man-made machine is aware of the world or of itself. It knows nothing of colour or meaning.

Does the artist have deeper insights into mind, than anatomists and physiologists and hardware and software computer engineers? One might say that artists view, and express, mind from the *inside*. This can hardly be claimed for physiologists, applying physical principles; yet they handle and understand the components that make our inner worlds.

A most important feature of perception – of the brain's ability to make sense of limited signals from the senses – is perception's power to *project* colour and meaning into the world of objects. It is truly a deep question, how much of our experience is *received* from the senses and what is *created* by the brain, though apparently out there. Both Isaac Newton and John Locke appreciated that colours are brain-created; so the object world would lack all colour and all sound without effective brains, and eyes and ears. This is still a shocking thought. Common sense has been shocked by science; though after three hundred years it is still not generally known that colours and sounds are products of brains, and they still seem to be out there belonging to objects.

How shocking should this get? Is *all* meaning created by brains and projected into an arid world? When resonating with works of art, are we responding to the artists' received insights of reality or to their brain-projections of meaning? Evidently, each of us creates our own realities. Science shocks common sense assumptions; yet it is this dialogue, together with increasing powers of technology to explain and to cure ills, that is so exciting and so promising for the future.

In this ambitious exhibition we are privileged to see discoveries and inventions at the heart of medicine – which uniquely combines objectivity of physical sciences with subjective

Head on

art with the brain in mind

Caterina Albano, Ken Arnold and Marina Wallace

 Wallace Kemp art@kt

A Wellcome Trust Exhibition

THE WELLCOME TRUST

Head on: art with the brain in mind

Caterina Albano, Ken Arnold and Marina Wallace

Medicine in context

Medicine is based on scientific curiosity and wonder; but it also relates to much in people's everyday lives. *Head On* is the first in a series of exhibitions put on at the Science Museum that look at aspects of this balance between medical science and its social and cultural context through a mixture of scientific, artistic and historical exhibits.

In collaboration with the Science Museum the Wellcome Trust seeks through these shows to raise awareness of biomedical science and how it affects people's lives, today and in the past. Many of the objects on show come from the Wellcome Collections, originally gathered by Sir Henry Wellcome and now mainly kept in the Wellcome Library for the History and Understanding of Medicine and in the Science Museum. Other objects from this collection can be seen in other galleries in the Science Museum, and at the Wellcome Library.

The Mission of the Wellcome Trust is to foster and promote research in order to improve human and animal health.

compassion for hurt bodies and minds. As medicine is effective, so we accept that it embodies important truths. More predictably, and perhaps more powerfully than the techniques of artists, medical technologies can switch minds on and off and change them by acting on the brain. Possibly anaesthesia is a key to understanding consciousness, by scientific methods of switching on and off underlying systems.

Do we discover processes of mind by seeing what changes mind, rather as physicists probe the nature of matter to discover its inner secrets? Known to antiquity - minds can be inspired and confused by rhetoric, and amused and fooled by conjuring. There are almost too many ways to affect mind. No doubt the brain sciences will come to impose discipline. Now that we can see, with wonderful technologies, which regions of brain 'light up' when we move a finger, or think, or imagine - can we at last relate physical structures of the brain to mind?

Surely there is little philosophical point in knowing which parts light up, without appreciating how these parts work. To appreciate functions carried out by brain mechanisms, to produce movement and thinking and imagining, or whatever, we need theoretical models of brain function. Surely this is as true for living brains as for understanding Babbage's machine, of brass and steel. Studying the mechanisms, may lead to very different-looking principles - here principles of mind. No doubt these will look like pictures of anatomy; yet, if the history of science is a true guide, it is the patient work of observation and experiment, and leaps of imagination for inventing hypotheses to explain, which with controlled experiments will lead to inner secrets of mind. Here, in this exhibition, we can see for ourselves routes taken by these explorers through the ages - pointing to future understanding of what goes on in our heads.

Richard Gregory CBE FRS
Emeritus Professor of Neuropsychology,
University of Bristol

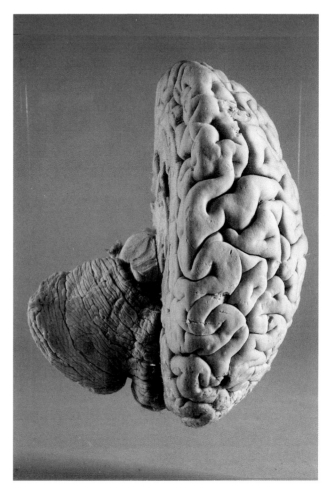

Charles Babbage's *Left cerebral hemisphere (half his brain)*, labelled 'Homo'
Hunterian Museum, Royal College of Surgeons, ref. RCSHM/D 685, part 2

David Hockney: The indoor eye

Lecturing in Florence, David Hockney (accompanied by Jan van Eyck's bespectacled cleric) demonstrates the formation of 'photographic' images using only a concave mirror. Like the retinal image, the picture formed in the dark room (the *camera obscura*) is upside down. Hockney believes that such optical projections were widely used by painters over the ages.

David Hockney
Portrait of Brad Bontems
Pencil and gouache on white paper
using a mirror-lens projection
2000
© David Hockney

Head on: art with the brain in mind

Caterina Albano, Ken Arnold and Marina Wallace

It weighs 1.5 kg and contains 28 billion cells, with a mind-boggling ten thousand billion connections between them. We each have one, and yet they are all different. While we are alive, they are constantly switched 'on'; turning them 'off' kills us. And from this extraordinary physical object comes the totality of our experiences, feelings, ideas, and understandings. Even our comprehension of what any of this might mean resides there.

Little wonder then that the human brain has long proved an irresistible magnet for curiosity and wonder, for investigation and speculation – particularly by artists and scientists. However, it is worth remembering in passing that for much of the early history of inquiries into the mind, the study of the brain seemed an irrelevance. Aristotle, for example, was far more concerned with the heart. But the growing focus on the brain in the last few centuries has led to its becoming increasingly fetishised. The brains of the famous, and especially of the famously brainy, have been subjected to particularly close scrutiny. That of the mathematical genius and inventor of the computer Charles Babbage, for example, was studied and kept (in 2 halves) by the Royal College of Surgeons. Without an institutional home, Einstein's brain received similar if less tidy treatment.

In recent years, the scientific study of the brain has undergone breath-taking advances. Research into neural networks has developed in conjunction with areas of computer science; great strides have been made in understanding prominent brain diseases such as stroke, Parkinson's and Alzheimer's. Questions about the role of language in thought, cognition and behaviour have spawned new fields of neurolinguistics and neuropsychology. And post-Freud, the exploration of the unconscious alongside the conscious mind has led to any number of therapeutic disciplines and medical strategies, not to mention the pharmaceutical industry's production of numerous mind-altering drugs. The last decade has also seen the successful transplantation of parts of the brain, and the production of devices that enable brain waves to run machinery. Finally and more controversially, some scientists have asserted that anatomy and brain-imaging are beginning to yield real advances in the comprehension of consciousness itself. Others of a more sceptical disposition contend instead that this work inevitably simplifies and even downgrades human behaviour in order to study it scientifically, leaving relatively untouched the most significant aspects of consciousness.

THE PHYSIOGNOMIST.

Published by C. Tilt, Fleet Street. 1831.

George E. Madeley, after G. Spratt *A physiognomist whose body is made up of faces, sitting at a table diagnosing people's physiognomic characteristics with the help of a book*
Coloured lithograph by George E. Madeley after G Spratt, 1831
Wellcome Library, ref. 3510i

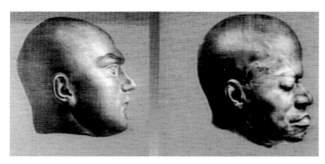

For just as long, the brain and mind have been subject to artistic scrutiny and exploration. Indeed, it has been argued that the emergence of cave-art in Europe some 30,000 years ago provides our most compelling evidence for the development of the human capacity to symbolise and communicate. Artists have always been concerned with issues about how we sense and imprint with meaning the world around us. Semir Zeki has gone so far as to propose that artists be thought of as neurologists of a different sort, "studying the brain with techniques that are unique to them and reaching interesting but unspecified conclusions about the organization of the brain." More interested in personal revelation than demonstrable and repeatable results, wave after wave of artists – impressionists, expressionists, pointillists, fauvists, surrealists, cubists, and so on – have experimented with alternate ways of understanding our sensory relationship with the world.

Led by contemporary art works, *Head On* draws on both these traditions, and especially on those moments when one has seemed relevant and significant for the other, in order to tease out some of the intriguing aspects of this most extraordinary thing – the brain. The exhibition is organised around three broad themes: the anatomy of the brain, models of the mind, and the relationship between the inside and outside of the head.

The bits of the brain

After the Renaissance, scientific studies of the human mind focused on the brain. But what was it composed of and how did it work? The development of the idea of understanding things by cutting them up into constituent sections led researchers to put the brain under the anatomist's knife. Many techniques were subsequently invented for dissecting, colouring and preserving specimens. Scientists also wondered about the relationship between the physical brain and the mind. For the seventeenth-century French philosopher René Descartes and his numerous followers, the answer lay in mechanical theories. The material that made up the mind worked like a machine, which somehow produced the immaterial stuff of thoughts and feelings.

In the mid-nineteenth century methods of studying the mind and brain were developed based on observing people with head injuries and illnesses. This led a number of researchers starting with Paul Broca to speculate that localised brain regions or centres were responsible for specific mental functions. A particular initial focus was on language, but the same approach has been extensively elaborated over the last 150 years.

The anatomical idea of looking at bits of the brain was pursued in ever-finer detail, with nineteenth-century researchers looking at biological tissue under achromatic microscopes uncovering the 'cell of thought': the neurone. Camillo Golgi's work on cells in the nervous system in the 1870s and Santiago Ramón y Cajal's further researches lay the foundations for a new, neurological era of brain research.

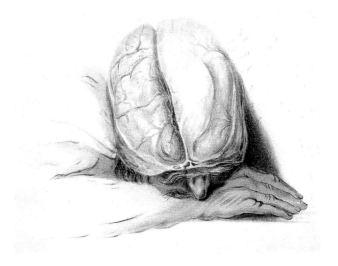

Charles Bell *The anatomy of the Brain Explained in a Series of Plates (1823)*   Plate I, Section of the Brain, original watercolour
Wellcome Library, ref. Western MS 1121

J. F. Gautier d'Agoty *Subcutaneous blood vessels of the head and neck* Colour mezzotints by J.F. d'Agoty after himself 1745–48
(Paris: Sieur Gautier) Wellcome Library, ref. 498088i

More recently, a series of powerful imaging techniques has given scientists windows through which to peer at normal functioning brains, without damaging them. Electroencephology-graphy (EEG), discovered in 1875, allowed detection of the brain's electrical signals in action. A century later, Computerised Axial Tomography (CAT) using multiple x-rays to build up images of brain structure, was invented. Today, Positron Emission Tomography (PET) and functional Magnetic Resonance Imaging (fMRI) further allows blood-flow in the brain to be viewed while subjects perform specific tasks. Like elements in a cubist painting, each method has added to the overall picture of the workings of the mind. But picturing what our brains are like and how they function still leaves the visible surface of the head a mystery. What about our faces and skulls - how do they relate to what goes on within?

From face and form to character

The links between the insides and outsides of the human head have for centuries intrigued both artists and scientists. In art, the portrait has been extensively used to pursue the question. Starting at least with the work of Leonardo, the idea that the inner workings of the soul finds physical expression in the human face and body has provided an anchor for much Western art. While more recently, a strong tradition in modern portraiture has evolved around a psychological interest in the face.

The formal study of the face and its links with personality (physiognomy) also has ancient roots; but in the 18th century, it became part of a new 'science of man'. Louis-Jean-Marie Daubenton proposed in a 1764 publication that the 'occipital angle', a characteristic based on the relative positions and measurements of the vertebral column and cranium, constituted the unique aspect of humanity. Explicitly or not, all this work was underlain by the assumption of links between the physical and the moral: between faces and characters. By the nineteenth century, these ideas had become widely adopted by sociologists, criminologists and anthropologists.

The principles of comparative anatomy were also evident in the work of Joseph Gall. His theory of heads (phrenology) related brain-regions, and the bumps on people's skulls that housed them, to specific moral attributes. His classification system

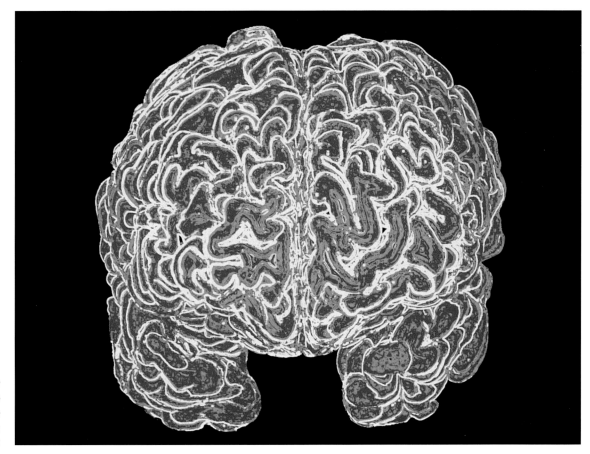

Heidi Cartwright
Coloured image of the anterior aspect of the human brain
Wellcome Photo Library

involved some 27 primitive forces – from an instinct for cruelty to the perception of colour, from a sense of humour to the faculty of imitating. Phrenology provided the basis for a huge range of societies, entertainments and consultations, which continued to be popular, though not scientifically supported, well into the 20th century. However, the idea of a modular mind – of allocating specific human characteristics and functions to particular neuro-anatomical regions – has continued ever since. Much of human 'personality', for example, is thought to originate in the frontal lobes, with memory being strongly associated with the hippocampus; while brain scans regularly identify bits that 'light up' when a subject moves a finger or becomes sexually aroused.

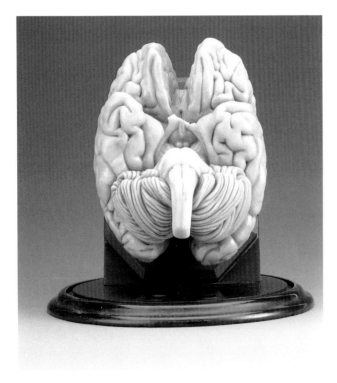

Joseph Towne *Wax model of a dissection of a brain*
1860s – 1870s
Hunterian Museum, Royal College of Surgeons, ref. S208

Right:
Richard Wentworth *Twenty seven minutes, twenty two nouns, seven adjectives* Book, assorted materials on mirror glass 1999
Lisson Gallery

Metaphors for the mind

So is the mind like a house full of rooms then: intelligence in the study, motion in the garage and sex in the bathroom? This is clearly a powerful metaphor; but it is only one amongst many that have gained currency, only then to be dropped in favour of another. Models and metaphors have in fact been crucial to both the artistic and scientific probing of the brain.

Mind-metaphors have sometimes come from nature and religion (a tree or a spirit), but more frequently from cutting-edge technology. Thus the invention of printing made the book and particularly the completeness of an encyclopaedia or a dictionary a compelling model of the mind. And as Richard Wentworth's work 'Twenty seven minutes, twenty two nouns, seven adjectives' suggests, book-marks are a powerful symbol of the mind at work. The Renaissance development of anatomical research and the mentality that linked physical structure to function helped establish another particularly powerful and predictively sophisticated model of the brain as a thinking machine. In this vein early modern clockwork gave way to nineteenth-century steam engines, and later to telephone exchanges and holograms. Most recently, the brain has been likened to a computer, and now the whole internet.

Western models of the mind have extensively focused on memory, often using analogies of words, pictures and collections: the mind as an alphabet, a slate or canvas, a cupboard or museum. After Freud, for whom memories came to have altogether more potent significance, the mind became a mystic writing pad. In art, thinking of the mind as a repository of the senses has proved extremely suggestive; while in some ways every artwork can be thought of as a model of the mind. Some sort of model, some metaphor or other, has then seemingly provided the starting point for every exploration of the mind – whether in art or science.

Head On tries throughout to make intriguing connections between the approaches of artists and scientists. Not concerned with the potential integration of their methodologies, nor with the supposed hidden beauty of science or the hidden rigour of art, the exhibition instead seeks inspiration in the overlaps and cross-overs between these different cultural approaches. Rarely presenting answers to any questions, *Head On* suggests instead that we might understand more by seeking than finding.

Right:
Ian Breakwell
In the wings
Photo-diptych
1993
Anthony Reynolds
Gallery

Elizabeth Frink
Desert Quartet I
Bronze, edition of 6
1989
Beaux Arts

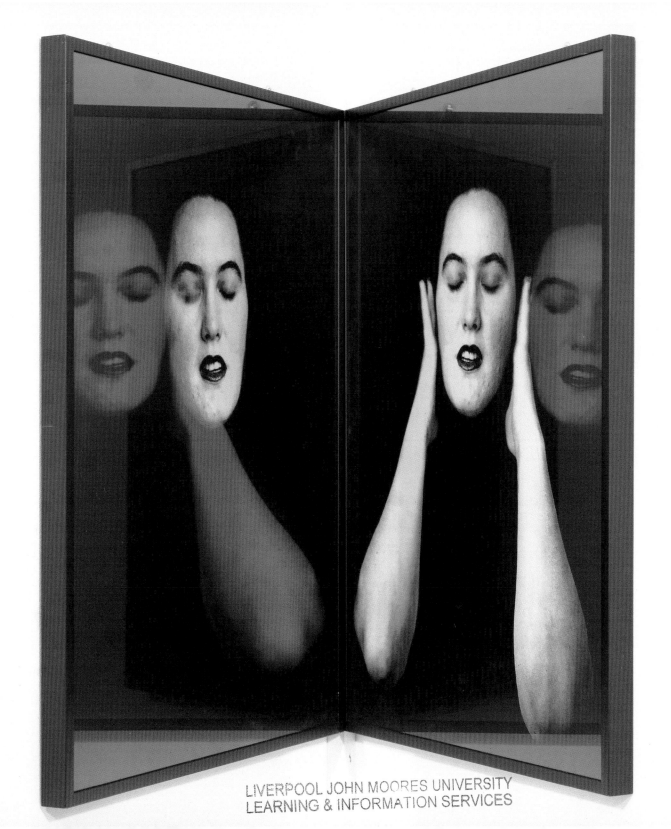

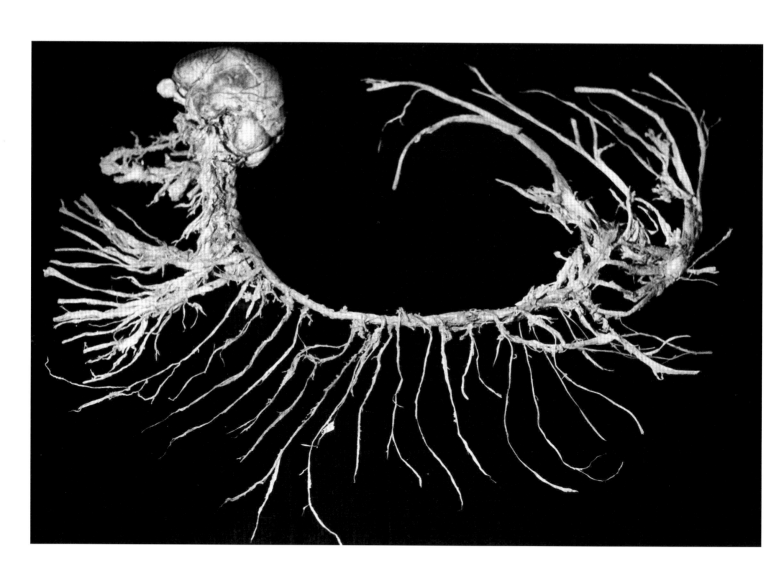

Pat York *Neural Nexus 2/5* Imbue print 2001
Image courtesy of the artist

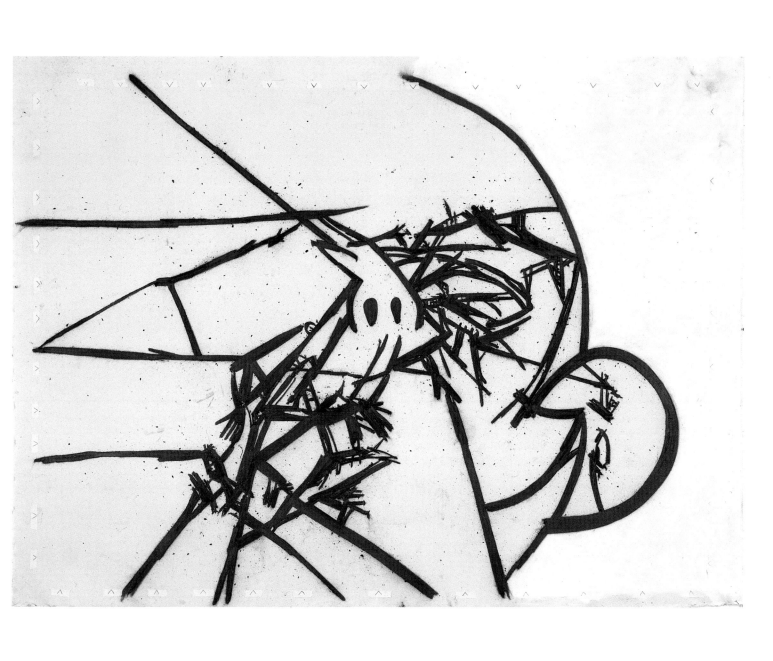

Tony Bevan   *Head PC008*   Acrylic on canvas   2000
Michael Hue-Williams Fine Art Gallery

Artists and scientists: meetings of minds

Caterina Albano, Ken Arnold and Marina Wallace

From the viewpoint of contemporary art, visual representations in brain sciences such as the psychology of perception, neurology and cognition have acquired a particular freshness and immediacy. This freshness is guaranteed by the freedom of the images (as in other sciences) from the ready-packaged theories and practices of the art world. A significant number of contemporary artists have chosen to conduct their practice at least in part through procedures of investigation and experimentation that refer to the world of science. More often than not they use processes which echo those of scientists, albeit in a different cultural context, within different parameters and with different ends in view. Concurrently, a number of curators, conservators, and historians are developing their own practice through the promotion of active relationships between artists and scientists. Those who operate judiciously in this field believe that it is crucial that new juxtapositions and parallels between the disciplines of art and science are created at a level that avoids opportunistic or approximate solutions. *Head On* was born from this conviction.

The points of contact established between the experiments of a number of neuro-scientists and psychologists and the researches of the eight contemporary artists selected for *Head On* have literally given shape to the sculptures, drawings, paintings and multi-media installations included in this exhibition. The historical objects on show are themselves in dialogue with the contemporary material, signalling the enduring basis of the processes of research in territories that have been of recurrent fascination throughout the ages

Two of the most significant of all general concepts which the artists and scientists in *Head On* have explored are those of the relationship between mind and body, and of the brain with the outside world. These are crucial questions, posed several times in the ancient world, and repeatedly in the 17th century, above all by Descartes, who famously postulated the separation of body and mind, world and spirit (*res extensa* and *res cogitans*). The problem of body and mind has also formed the basis of much recent philosophical speculation and scientific modelling, from

Putnam's and Turing's functionalist theories of the mind in the 1960s – linked to the development of computers – to more recent theories of neuro-science developed by Antonio Damasio, who has roundly denounced "Descartes' error". Damasio argues that the brain is not an entity separated from the body, but it is essentially one of the bodily organs, inextricably linked to their mechanisms and functions. As fundamental corollaries to such philosophically orientated investigations of the mind-body problem (though too often separated from them by disciplinary boundaries), the sciences of perception and cognition are in the process of redefining how the relationship between the brain and the outside world is understood.

Concerned as they are with ways of seeing, perceiving and representing the outside world, all eight of the *Head On* artists have, in their own way, and through different routes, tackled these perennial questions. Their accounts of their collaboration with scientists and of their own process of research, is included in the latter part of this publication, as "artists' logs". Our facilitation and monitoring of this process, as curators, and our provisional interpretation of it, is documented below. In a future project it would be fascinating to include the scientists' own accounts, with their reflections and insights, as a result of their collaborations with the artists.

"Hearing" and "Seeing": the physicality of consciousness

Annie Cattrell started her investigations with an acute curiosity about what she called the "physicality of consciousness", setting out to represent the "anatomical sites, within an individual brain, which mirror our experience of the outside world". Her modelling of the intricate and delicate nervous and respiratory systems – rendered by Cattrell in transparent glass or resin – trace the inner shape of the human body. When she turned to the brain and began speculating about the visual manifestation of thought and consciousness, her immediate points of reference were contemporary imaging techniques. She had her own brain

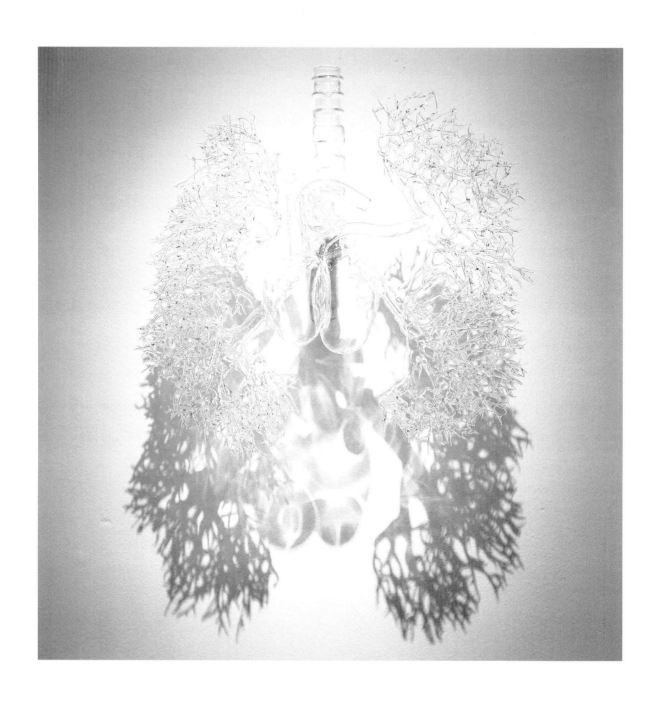

Annie Cattrell *Capacity* Glass 2000
Image courtesy of the artist

Annie Cattrell Wax mould of activity in a section of the brain, used for rapid prototyping

scanned, and pinned the fMRI (functional Magnetic Resonance Imaging) images up in her studio, seeking insight from the scientific visual conventions and trying to formulate her own visualisation of brain imaging. As a sculptor she eventually found that her answer did not lie in the imagery of the scans but in a three-dimensional rendering of selected areas of the brain. To realise her vision, she collaborated with the scientists who use a technique called Rapid Prototyping (RP) which transcribes fMRI data of the brain's activity into startling 3D cerebral maps. Intrigued by the process of RP, Cattrell retained a number of the grey-coloured wax moulds, which uncannily resemble modern urban landscapes.

The objects she produced are shown embedded in blocks of transparent resin, and are visual presentations of the activity of the sensory areas of sight and hearing of a particular person, a sort of three-dimensional, mental finger print. She is rendering

Annie Cattrell *Seeing* Resin encapsulated in hot cure resin 2001

Image courtesy of the artist

Annie Cattrell *Hearing*   Resin encapsulated in hot cure resin   2001
Image courtesy of the artist

Andrew Carnie   Image from *Magic Forest*: slide dissolve work   2001
Sponsored by Kodak   Image courtesy of the artist

in three dimensions the physical evidence of brain activity that the artist had been seeking in the scans. "Hearing" and "Seeing" work hand-in-hand with current scientific theories of localisation within the brain, teasing the brain apart visually and deconstructing its familiarly enigmatic, monolithic, opaque and convoluted shape. Joseph Towne's 19th century wax sculptures of literally "opened" heads with portraits of protruding brains provide telling juxtapositions to Cattrell's elegant, conceptualised sculptures.

Magic Forest: cells and neurones

Andrew Carnie, whose initial training was in biology, has for long been fascinated with the properties of memory. His work, which generally refers to memory through visual metaphors such as suitcases, found a new vehicle for expression when he was exposed, in scientific laboratories, to the visual intricacies of neuronal proliferation, migration, synapsis, connectivity, and apoptosis (cell death). He encountered images of living brain cells as viewed through a laser scanning confocal microscope and documented with the aid of computer imaging. Carnie's historical points of reference were the experiments by the pioneering nineteenth-century anatomist Santiago Ramon Y Cajal, who stained thin resin-impregnated slices of the brain, using a process invented by Camillo Golgi. Cajal was looking for cell distribution, aiming to establish a visual model for the cellular composition of the brain, at the time thought to be made up of a continuous mesh of interconnected fibres. The scientist was intuitively reaching out towards the early twentieth-century discovery of the fine structure of neurones. Carnie, moved by the eloquence of Cajal's own drawings, attempted to represent the wonder of the recent scientific images that he witnessed, without losing sight of older and imaginative representations of the intricate and delicate "forest" inside the topography of our brains.

"Magic Forest" is a large, walk-in installation of images drawn by the artist with computer-aided techniques. His images are projected from opposite sides of a darkened room through layers of suspended fabric. The installation evokes the fragility and fluidity and the extraordinary speed of the development and interconnectivity of brain cells. "Magic Forest" specifically tells of his reaction to the representation on a very

TRAM DEPOT
GALLERY

ANDREW CARNIE

25

AGE 7-9

Word
puzzles

YOUR CHILD CAN BE A
GENIUS

Q

Cover of an educational CD-ROM for children ages 7–9   2000

fine scale of neural anatomy and neuronal migration in relation to the genetic patterning of the brain as it matures. Thinking, like Cattrell, about the transformation of sections into three-dimensional models, he points out that "today, our understanding of the brain still requires the imaginative and computer-aided analysis of slices through brain tissue. By using fluorescent dyes, slices no longer have to be collected using a sharpened blade". In the quest for 3-D understanding, new technologies are extending the visual possibilities: "Laser scanning confocal microscopes can capture sections of stained neurones optically, giving unprecedented images of the three-dimensional living brain cells retained within computer memory."

You have five seconds: words and images

Katharine Dowson's interest in brain functions and in current theories of localisation stems from her experience of having been diagnosed with dyslexia as a child. As a particular condition of brain performance, dyslexia has a short diagnostic history. Until the late 1960s children who displayed difficulties with processes such as writing, reading or following instructions correctly, were deemed to be of lesser intelligence. Intelligence tests, pioneered by Alfred Binet in France in 1905, continued to be used, until recently, to test children with reading and writing difficulties. Particularly in the field of education, in Western culture visual skills have generally been valued less than verbal,

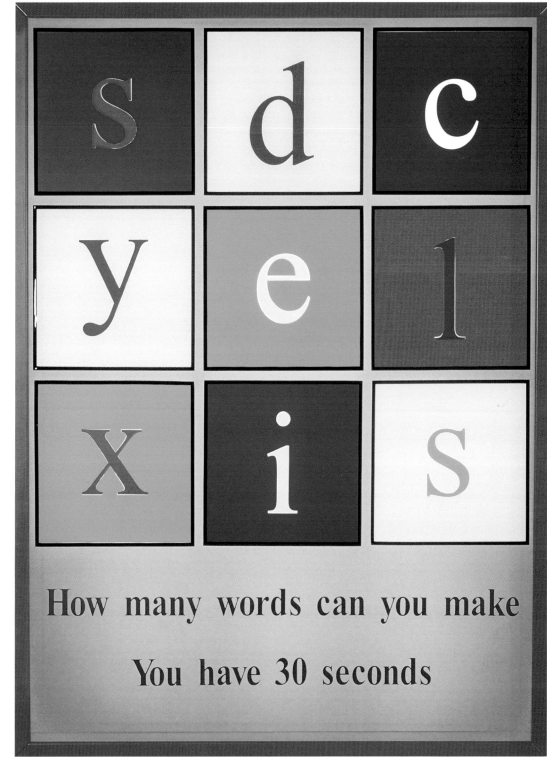

How many words can you make

You have 30 seconds

Katharine Dowson
Dyslexics
Acrylic, aluminium light box
2001

logical and mathematical skills. Dowson found that IQ tests designed in the 1950s and 1960s, betrayed this bias in their design. Her sensitivity to the visual field has guided her through a series of experiments using verbal puzzle games such as Scrabble, Boggle, Hangman, and crosswords. She has conducted her own visual experiments in dialogue with neuroscientists and psychologists who are researching into language processes located in particular areas of the brain, and into current theories of the genetic transmission of dyslexia. Whilst devising her contributions to *Head On*, Dowson took part in a series of scientific experiments, having her brain scanned in controlled situations.

The resulting works fall into three categories. The first work is constructed from old form boards of word-search games arranged by the artist so as to spell the words associated with the frustration of being dyslexic. The second comprises large wall-mounted visual interpretations of IQ tests, spelling out the frustration of being given the command of finding the solution within a few seconds or being falsely reassured that "this shouldn't be difficult". The last provides a visual representation of her own dyslexic self, a puzzle made of cubes with pictures of her own chromosomes, alluding both to children's games and to current theories about the genetic inheritance of dyslexia.

"Things that we think we see when we don't. Things that we do see when we think we don't."

Questions of visual perception are variously explored by Claude Heath and Tim O'Riley, one by denying sight, the other by exploring binocular vision.

The translation of a three dimensional experience into a two-dimensional representation is central to both artists.

Claude Heath uses his body and brain as an extension of sight, but draws blindfolded. He touches the three dimensional object (often a sculpture of a head, frequently that of his own brother Toby) without seeing it, and produces marks on paper in a systematic way, visually mapping the route of his tactile experience and its connection to the brain. His work is essentially process-based, with an outcome which is literally unforeseen until completion (since he remains blindfolded until the very end of the drawing). He starts the drawing from a fixed point at the top of the head, marking this spot with a piece of blue tack

both on the sculpture and on the piece of paper. The artist's hand repeatedly returns to the piece of blue tack as a point of reference; the rest is "felt" and "remembered" through the hand and the brain in concert, in a way that resonates with Damasio's dissolution of the mind-body schism. The finished work on canvas is a transposition of the original experimental drawing, translated onto canvas or board using pricked paper and pouncing.

Through his collaboration with neuro-scientists and psychologists experimenting with eye movement, in preparation for *Head On*, Claude Heath himself participated in a number of controlled experiments at University College, London. His interest in the head and in visual representation extends to the genetic inheritance of facial features and family resemblance. Together with his father and brother, he had his face scanned at the Galton Laboratory at University College. His drawings of Toby are a sort of extended visual-cum-tactile map of a face which has common characteristics with his own, both in external form and in genetic constitution.

Through investigations in binocular vision, Tim O'Riley explores the faculty of visual perception centring again on the relationship between the body and the brain, the outside three-dimensional world and its two-dimensional representation. He questions fundamentally the certainty of the direct correspondence between the outside world and its subjective representation by using visual "tricks" to lead us into a bidimensional illusion of a three dimensional world. In contrast to Claude Heath, who resorts to "old" art practices such as drawing by hand, pouncing and tracing, Tim O'Riley makes abundant use of new technologies. He does, however, refer directly back to old technologies, most notably the early nineteenth-century stereoscopic device invented by Charles Wheatstone, which was developed not so much for public entertainment as in the context of research into the nature of vision. Like Wheatstone's images, O'Riley's work present illusionism par excellence: his images give a sense of solidity and pretend to exist "in reality", proposing themselves as representations of an existing three-dimensional world. In fact, all O'Riley's worlds are invented, existing only in the images and not in any free-standing reality.

The artist uses sophisticated computer techniques – as sophisticated as a nineteenth century stereoscope was in its own day –

Claude Heath Overlay drawing for *Head Tilting Forward*, detail

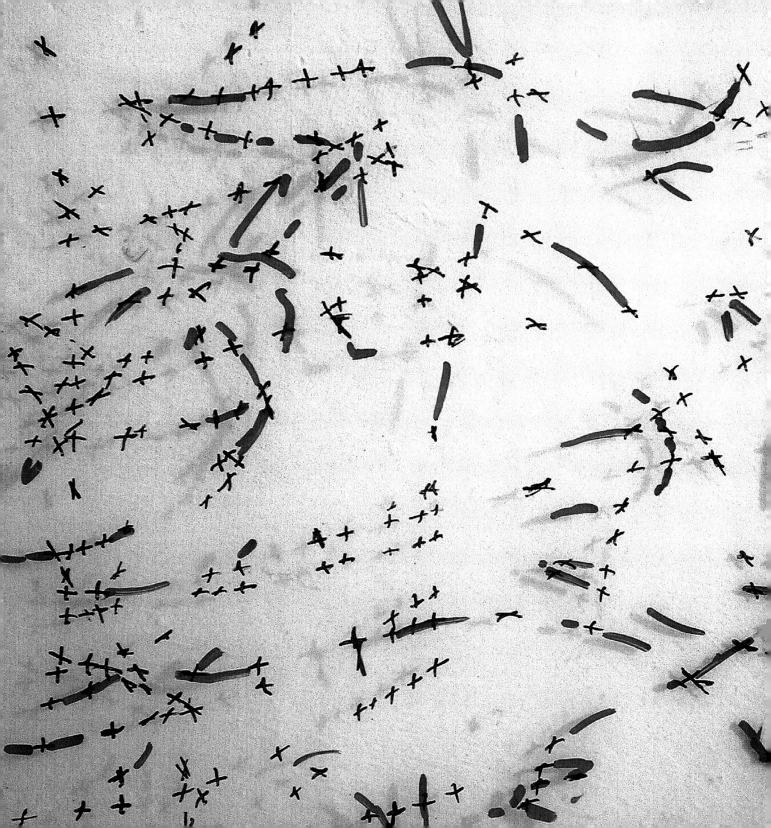

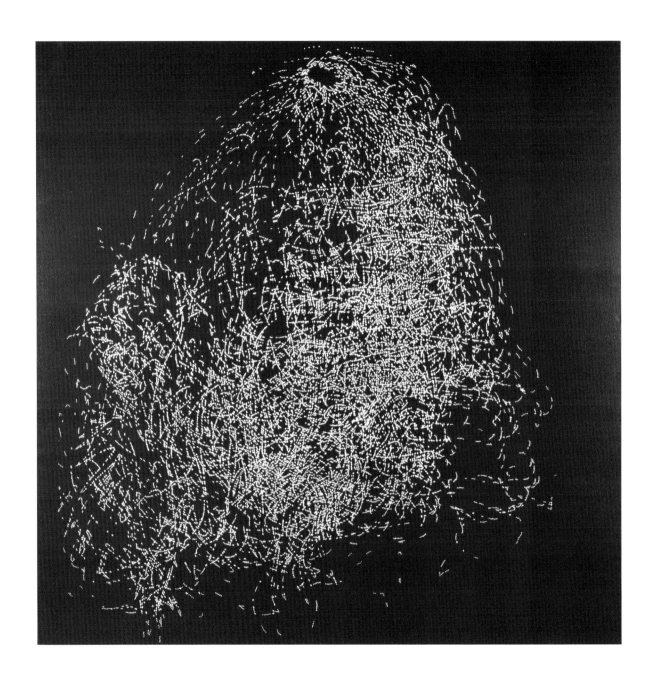

Claude Heath *Head Tilting Forward* Acrylic on linen 2001

Tim O'Riley *Galaxy* Digital c-print on aluminium 2001

which invite us to view two flat images that together appear solid and three-dimensional. The image appears solid; the artist writes:

> "This sense of solidity occurs somewhere in our brain and is not present in the pictures unless they are seen in the right way. What intrigues me about illusions in general, and stereo illusions in particular, is that they seem to raise a question about where exactly the picture is in relation to us when we look at it. Is it a property of the physical image or of our visual/mental system, or does it exist somewhere between the two, being both 'actual' and 'mental' simultaneously?" On a philosophical level he reflects that "in everyday life, we are constantly inferring whole things from fragments, interpreting and making sense – perceptually, emotionally, physically – out of the apparent randomness and disorder around us. Shared experiences enable us to make sure our consciousness corresponds to the outside world."

Just as Charles Wheatstone's early stereoscopic pictures, made just prior to the invention of photography, were hand-drawn images of simple, usually rectilinear objects (cubes, lines, steps), O'Riley himself uses simple geometric forms for his own computer generated images. For us, these geometric forms assume the look of a lamp, a book, a briefcase, a playing card.... After all, does not the whole of art production and visual representation more generally function as a trick of the mind? And, as the artist himself asks, "doesn't everything we perceive somehow occupy this mysterious territory, being in some a sense product of the constant negotiation that takes place between our internal reality and the external, physical world?"

During his collaborations with scientists for *Head On*, O'Riley was introduced to particular brain pathologies concerning the loss or augmentation of the visual field, such as visual neglect, visual extinction, hallucination and inattentional blindness. In his "log" he tells the story of a patient with visual neglect and its relevance to his own research into visual perception.

The "inner head": pathologies and culture

Much current knowledge in neuro-science is extracted from the study of pathologies. Letizia Galli's work, for many years, has been informed by concepts relating to psychotherapy, recovery and neurology. She devoted her research time for *Head On* to conversations with a number of psychiatrists and psychologists looking at anxiety and depressive disorders. The common definition of anxiety as a necessary alerting signal which warns us of impending danger and enables us to deal with the threat, excludes its pathological manifestation. In its pathological expression, anxiety is the product of misplaced human perceptions identifiable with specific physical dysfunctions, and is therefore especially relevant in terms of our present quest. As Damasio has argued, the complex integration of somatically expressed feelings, mental emotions and intellectual cognition requires that the brain is understood organically and physically as an integral part of the total body system. Pathological conditions of anxiety highlight precisely this integration of mind and body.

Through her conversations with neuroscientists at the Institute of Psychiatry in London, Letizia Galli established that anxiety, as a pathology, derives from a dysfunction in the cerebral cortex. She looked at the Obsessive–Compulsive (OC) syndrome, Behavioural Inhibition Systems (BIS) and panic disorders. In the exhibition she introduces the clinical aspect of neuro-science, and, like Katharine Dowson, provides an implicit, (and ironic) commentary on the culture of diagnosis and cure, with particular reference to psychiatry. Both artists wittily exploit a repertoire of apparently simple signposts to gain access to complex mental landscapes.

The cultural expression and modes of analysis encountered by Dowson and Galli are essentially framed by the premises of Western culture, above all our scientific concepts. It is with Osi Audu's work that we open the way to concepts of the head that are rooted in a non-Western world. Audu is intrigued by the relationship between brain and mind, and the concept of inner vision, the production of imagination, dream imagery, the storing of images, and memory recall. The artist uses, as his initial point of reference, fundamental concepts from his culture of origin, that of the Yoruba people of Nigeria. His contact with

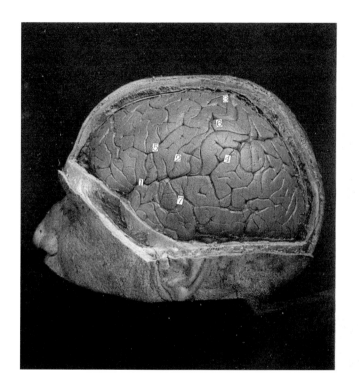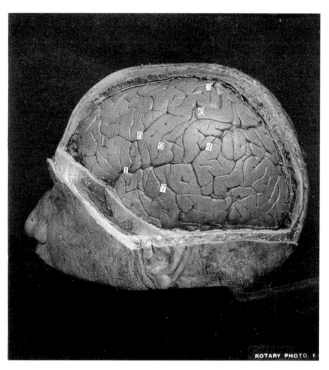

ROTARY PHOTO. E

Stereoscopic image No. 10   Cranial Cerebral Topography
(from The Edinburgh stereoscopic atlas of anatomy,edited by David Waterstone,
Edinburgh: T.C. & E.C. Jack, 1905–1906)
Wellcome Library, ref. icv 49466

scientists at University College London provided the basis for a dialogue on the scientific visualisation of neurone activity. MRI scans are a way of looking inside the living head. In Yoruba culture, the concept of the inner head is intimately related to that of the universe. What goes on inside the head, is connected to what goes on in the whole universe. Audu explains that "the Yoruba word for the head is 'ori'. The English translation for 'ori' is 'that which sees'."

The eye, which often appears in Audu's work, figures as a sign of consciousness. In his metal sculpture, "The Seeing Eye", which leans against a wall and resembles a silhouette on a human scale, the mechanical eye is operated by a sensor, opening and shutting as we approach or move away. The eye denotes a particular state of consciousness in the presence of an animate outside stimulus. When the eye is closed, another type of consciousness is implied, dependent upon memory and inner picturing.

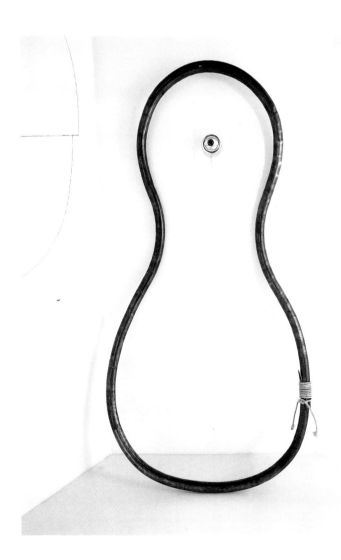

Osi Audu *The Seeing Mind*
Steel, rope, animatronic eye and perspex
2002

Gerhard Lang *Unbekannt, Phantombild* Identikit Photograph
2001 (work in progress)

synapses – provide an intuitive whole which is greater and more extensive in its ramifications than the mere sum of the parts.

At one level we may say that the art works in *Head On* owe much to the visual representations produced by and for scientists. It is also to be hoped that scientists' research will be enriched by the visual solutions produced by artists. At another level, beyond that of demonstrating immediate dialogue and influence, we intend that the exhibition in its whole and its parts will interact creatively with the spectator's experiences in ways that are both planned and unplanned. In the final analysis, the research fields conquered by the artists and scientists are not arcane subjects of specialist concern, but involve the way that we all confront the mind-body problem every moment of our waking and sleeping lives.

"Imago Cerebri I"

With Gerhard Lang's work we return to the seventeenth-century Western idea of the mind: Lang's "Imago Cerebri I" is, in many ways, an apt summary of past and present attempts to represent the mind, and is therefore an appropriate work with which to conclude *Head On*. But it also leaves the process conveniently open. The imagery is that of a cabinet within which each object can be moved or substituted by a surrogate, and where the relative relationships between the elements are still fluid. Lang worked closely with Professor Uta Frith, of the Department of Cognitive Neuroscience at University College, London. Through a series of conversations, they came jointly to devise the idea of producing an image of the brain in a metaphorical way. Their image of the brain is a "cabinet of curiosity" filled with various objects, the totality of which is but one step towards the totality of knowledge.

"Imago Cerebri I" includes a vast array of objects: a telescope, a dodecahedron, fossils, minerals, ancient Egyptian, Chinese, Indian and Greek artefacts, a stuffed owl, etc. In its diverse universality, it resembles some of the earliest wunderkammern, which were assembled philosophically as "microcosms" of the universe and as miniature palaces of memory. As in all effective collections, the suggestive mental connections between the discrete items in Lang's assemblage – the visual and intellectual

Gerhard Lang *Unbekannt, Phantombild* Identikit Photograph
2002 (work in progress)

Osi Audu

Title of Work/s:

Conscious and Unconscious Mind
Steel and yellow rope   2002

Outer and Inner Head
Acrylic and wool on canvas (diptych)
2002

The Seeing Mind
Steel, rope, animatronic eye and
perspex   2002

Historical Material:

Wooden chair, stained black. Congo
Science Museum, n.d. (ref. A 602179)

Ntutu Agwu group effigy, with back
to back figures of a male and female
(with child in her arms). Carved
wood. Ibo people, Southern Nigeria,
1870 – 1930

Science Museum (ref. A 657365)

Small carved kneeling female figure
with five infants. Hardwood, mirror
and glass. Possibly Bakongo people.
Congo, 1850 – 1920
Science Museum (ref. A652609)

Project Statement:

The Yoruba word for the head is 'ori'.
The English translation for 'ori' is
'that which sees'.

Project Development:

I am interested in this notion that
perception is central to the head and
indeed to human consciousness. For
this exhibition project – Head On –
I am exploring the phenomenon of
inner vision. I am intrigued by the
brain-mind processes through which
images of the visible world are perceived, and how these neurological
processes can trigger or participate
in conjuring other inner images such
as an after-image, images in dreams,
and the recall of images in memory.
I feel that this process of engaging
with an inner image could be seen
as a reference to an 'inner head', or,
to use the Yoruba word, 'ori inu'
which is seen as the seat of consciousness. I am also exploring the divide
between the conscious and unconscious mind, looking at how parts
of the neurons in the brain light up
during MRI scanning to indicate
conscious experience.

The Seeing Mind
The sensor triggers the eye to open
when a spectator moves close to the
work.

In this piece, I am exploring the
idea that perception occurs, not in
the eyes, but in the mind, through
the eyes.

Outer and Inner Head
An optical 'illusion' occurs as the
viewer transfers his or her gaze from
the left panel to the right panel. An
after-image is formed in the viewer's
mind's eye. It would appear as if the
eye has a mind of its own. This visual
echo, an intangible yet real image, is
seen as a reference to the nature of
consciousness or the 'inner head'.

Conscious and Unconscious Mind
Inspired by the way neurons light
up during MRI scanning to indicate
conscious experience, in this piece
I am looking at the contrast and
similarity between the conscious
and the unconscious mind.

As a contextual reference for my
work I have found the three historical
artefacts from The Science Museum
ethnographic collection quite
interesting.

Acknowledgements:
I would like to thank the following
for their support:

Prof. Christopher Kennard, Imperial
College School of Medicine; Nasira
Sheikh-Miller, Science Communica-
tion & Collections, Science Museum.

**Osi Audu's references
include:**
Audu, Osi, 'The Body is a Headrest:
  another look at the Phenomenon
  of Consciousness.' Paper presented
  at the conference on The Human
  Image at the British Museum,
  17 – 19 January 2001

Gaudion, A., On The Fringe Review:
  Osi Audu, 'tooth fairy tales',
  13 October 2000, www.newswatch.
  co.uk/entertainment/theatre/
  37065

Mack, J., *Africa – Arts and Cultures*,
  2000, British Museum Press.
  pp. 28 – 29

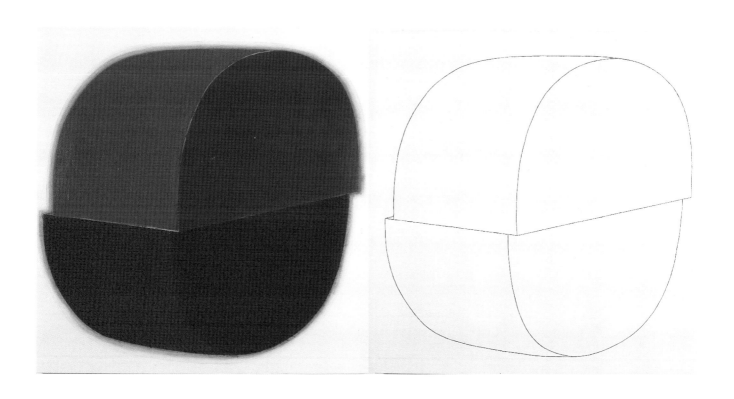

Osi Audu *Outer and Inner Head* Acrylic and wool on canvas 2002

Annie Cattrell

Title of Work/s:

Seeing
Resin encapsulated in hot cure resin
2001

Hearing
Resin encapsulated in hot cure resin
2001

Historical Material:

Joseph Towne, Wax model of
an un-dissected brain, 1860–70s
Gordon Museum

Joseph Towne, Wax model of
a dissected brain of a baby (whole),
1860–70s
Gordon Museum

Joseph Towne, Wax model of
a dissected brain of a baby, cut
hemispherically, 1860–70s
Gordon Museum
Joseph Towne, Wax model of
a magnified brain with section
of the eye, 1860–70s
Gordon Museum

Joseph Towne, Wax model of
a dissection of the head and neck
1860–70s
Gordon Museum

Joseph Towne, Wax model of
a dissection of a brain, 1860–70s
Hunterian Museum, Royal College
of Surgeons (ref. S 208)

Project Statement:

There are a vast number of anatomical sites within the individual
brain which mirror our experience
of the outside world. When looking
or listening, for example, certain
areas of the brain can be shown to
be active, and reveal the shape, location and volume of activity of the
senses. In *Hearing* and *Seeing*, fMRI
data was transcribed into three
dimensions through a laser engineering process called Rapid
Prototyping. These cerebral maps
are not templates (as in

Phrenology): they reveal the actual
uniqueness of the person (like a fin-
gerprint), and the physicality of
thought.

Project Development:

I became particularly interested in
the functioning of the brain while
I was artist in residence at the Royal
Edinburgh Hospital (Edinburgh's
main Psychiatric Hospital) during
1990–91. Mental illness holds many
stigmas which differ profoundly
from attitudes towards physical illness. I began considering the brain
as a physical entity made of similar
constituents as every aspect of the
corporeal body. Through childhood
the brain develops and grows
according to our genetic makeup as
well as our experience of the outside
world. This delicate dialogue between
the exterior world and our individual
interior blueprint became the
beginning of my fascination about
the brain and what makes us who
we are, and what is self – perhaps
consciousness?

Spring 2000

The initial work on the making of
Hearing and *Seeing* began when I was
asked to do a short residency at the
Camden Arts Centre (funded by the
Gulbenkian Foundation). I explored
the idea that the brain has specific
regions that locate the sites of the
senses, emotions and memory (I
was reading *Consciousness Explained*
by Daniel C. Dennett, *Descartes' Error*
by Antonio R.Damasio, *Mapping the
Mind* by Rita Carter, and *The Human
Brain* by Susan Greenfield). I became
interested in the relationship
between what is a physical entity (i.e.
the gray matter within the brain or
the musculature of the body) and

what are in effect the locations of
thought/mind. Digital information
reveals an activation of the living
brain by isolating and mapping
the location of the activated cortex
making the brain reveal that it is
alive and contains detectable activity
(for example, the oxygen within the
blood). External stimulus (such as
sound or smell) travels through the
primary sensing systems to deep
within the brain, generating the
potential for neurological activation
and growth. Our genetic makeup
and this growth activity help to
form the self – the individual's core
persona.

Summer 2000

Max Davison (Artist and Senior
Lecturer at the Royal College of Art)
introduced me to state of the art
technology called Rapid Prototyping
(RP) and the American company 3D
Systems who manufacture this processing in Hemel Hempstead (they
offered to provide sponsorship). The
RP process is usually only used in
engineering or in very expensive and
life-threatening medical conditions
in order for the surgeon to identify
tumors or growths within a patient's
brain for precise understanding
of the pathology before a brain
operation. RP is a technique whereby
three dimensional computer information (stereolithography) is trans-
ferred through laser technology into
a variety of different materials: wax,
resin and nylon – making what is
virtual into a real object. It was my
aim to transfer functional MRI brain
scans, which reveal the anatomy of
the senses, into Rapid Prototyped
volumes. These sculptures isolate the
mental activity of thoughts from the
rest of the brain and make it visible

in three dimensions, revealing the anatomy of a thought or a sense which can also allow an understanding of the brain as an organ in a constant state of flux. The fMRI scan data and the translation of that data into three dimensions (through the RP technique) is the equivalent of a literal casting (without touch) – making solid a transient moment of the shape of thought within the brain.

Autumn 2000

While I was Arts Council of England Helen Chadwick Fellow (based at Oxford University), I was introduced to Baroness Susan Greenfield by Paul Bonaventura from the Laboratory (Ruskin School of Fine Art and Drawing): we talked about if and how consciousness could be visualised. I met Dr Steve Smith (who is a brain imaging specialist at FMRIB at Oxford University) who provided me with data showing auditory and visual activation within the human brain. Mr Teddy (neurosurgeon at the Radcliffe Hospital and Fellow of St Peters College) discussed the intricacies of brain surgery and the possibility of me watching him at work. Dr Mark Lythgoe (neuro-physiologist from the Institute of Child Health Care at Great Ormond Street Hospital in London) and I began to work together to combine the digital data from Dr Steve Smith into compatible files (STL) for the RP process.

Dr Lythgoe sourced the relevant software and rendered the fMRI data into virtual models.

Winter 2000–01

Once the exacting translating process was complete 3D Systems (Colin Blain European Applications Specialist) manufactured *Seeing* and *Hearing* using the RP resin technique. The models were then encapsulated into transparent resin sponsored by Hobarts Ltd (Brian Cain technical director). The first showing of these two works was at the Anne Faggionato Gallery in London during March 2001. Working closely with scientists and in particular Dr Mark Lythgoe gave me a new context in which to discuss and test ideas about thinking of the brain as a physical entity, its constituent components and if the activity of thinking and thoughts can be made visible. Dr Mark Lythgoe and I have been planning to continue to work together, researching further work on the physical rendering of all of the senses.

Acknowledgments:

Dr Mark Lythgoe and Dr Steve Smith, Great Ormond Street Hospital; Max Davison, Royal College of Art; Colin Blain, 3D Systems; Brian Cain, Hobarts Ltd.

Annie Cattrell
Wax mould: obtained through the Rapid Prototyping (RP) process

Andrew Carnie

Title of Work/s:

Magic Forest: slide dissolve work
Two projectors, time dissolve unit,
160 slides, three gauze screens,
aluminium supporting bars, two
plinths 2001
Sponsored by Kodak, Arts and
Humanities Research Board, and
The Faculty of Arts, Southampton
University.

Historical material:

Santiago Ramon y Cajal, *Neuronismo
o reticularismo? Las pruebas objetivas
de la unidad anatomica de la celulas
nerviosas* (Madrid: Archivos de neuro-
biologìa, v. 13, 1933) Figs 157–158,
159–160. Neurones
Wellcome Library (ref. Med. XWL)

Santiago Ramon y Cajal, *Recuerdos de
mi vida* (Madrid: Impr. de J. Pueyo,
1923) Fig. 4a–5a. Neurones
Wellcome Library (ref. Med. Hist2
BZP Ramon)

Project Statement:

The project has become a way of
exploring, through sculpture and
time-based work, recent develop-
ments in the understanding of the
structure and growth of neurones
in the brain. The work is based on
contemporary concepts of neuronal
proliferation, migration, connectivity,
and cell death (apoptosis). Visually
owing much to looking at optical
sections of the structure of the brain,
the work started as an examination
of memory. The brain structure holds
memories: the work reflects some
recent findings about the slow drift
of memory and the processing that
happens over years to fix memories
through dreams. *Magic Forest* reflects
the state of flux, fluidity and change
that is revealed through contemporary neuroscience. The work pays
homage to the beauty and sheer
complexity of the structure of the
brain and its steady development, its
genetically-driven growth influenced
by experience.

Project Development:

The work has developed out of:

· the sheer complexity and beauty
revealed by the confocal microscope,
the fluorescent stained sections, *in
vitro* samples changing and developing
over time. This marks a change in
science from morbid anatomy to the
appreciation of developing structures.

· the fragility, fluidity and speed of
the development of interconnectivity
revealed by the confocal microscope
and computer analysis.

· the fact that a chick egg is fertilised
(on day one), that the chick's body
and brain develop, and by day twenty
two the neurones are completely
organised so that on breaking from
the shell the young chick can see – it
all works, and it can see its mother.
The complexity of the signalling
systems that allow the millions of
neurones to find where they are
going and to develop in this way.

· recent work with MRI scanners
that reveals the effect that nurture
can have on the morphology of the
brain. Individuals' occupations mean
that their brains develop in different
ways. This restructuring goes on
after early brain development.

· recent work that shows memories
as electrical signals seeming to
pass back and forth between the
hippocampus and the cortex over
lengthy periods as they are fixed
into long term memory.

I have responded to the very complex
and overwhelming research that I
have witnessed. The research was
'overwhelming' in that I didn't
always understand the scientists'
specialist knowledge, the specific
results of which I found impossible
to covert into art work. It has been
a breathtaking experience.

   For *Magic Forest* I looked, in particular, at the work of Dr Richard
Wingate at the Medical Research
Centre for Developmental
Neurobiology, King's College,
London. His work is on fine-scale
neural anatomy and neuronal
migration in relation to genetic
patterning of the maturing brain.
On seeing the first version of *Magic
Forest* he tried to contextualise the
work in a piece titled "Slices, fragments and snapshots".

Wingate writes:
"The brain consists of millions of
neurones, each a finely branching
microscopic structure that reaches
out for near and distant neighbours.
They contribute to a distributed
circuitry whose logic remains one
of the greatest mysteries of biology.
Structure and function are synony-
mous. The geometry of the neurone
determines its interconnections and
is a physical manifestation of the
functional processing of the electrical
signals it receives. The complexity
and beauty of its structure also
reflects the developmental constraints
that shaped its growth.

   Over a hundred years ago, the
pioneer anatomist, Santiago Ramon
y Cájal, sliced up resin-impregnated
brains which had been stained by a
capricious potassium dichromate-
silver process invented by Camillo
Golgi. For reasons that are still not
fully understood, a few cells in a
thousand turn completely black,
their fine processes packed with
dense particles. By studying the
fragments of cell distributed through
the thin slices of brain, individual
neurones were imaginatively recon-
structed and giving rise to a model of
the cellular composition of different
brain regions, their interconnections
and even the direction of the flow of
information.

   Prior to Golgi's stain the very exis-
tence of cells in the brain was hotly
debated. Contrary evidence suggested
that the brain was a continuous
mesh of interconnected fibres – a

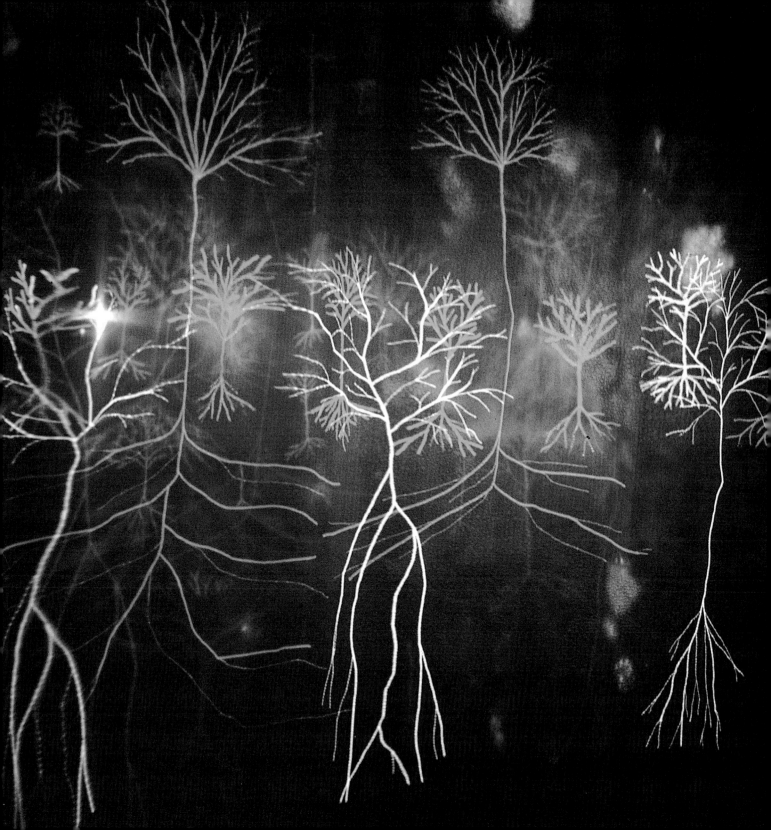

theory that was eventually superseded as the fine structure of neurones was uncovered in the early part of the twentieth century. Today, our understanding of the brain still requires the imaginative and computer-aided analysis of slices through brain tissue. By using fluorescent dyes, slices no longer have to be collected using a sharpened blade. Laser scanning confocal microscopes can capture sections of stained neurones optically, giving unprecedented images of the three-dimensional living brain cells retained within computer memory.

Just as our concepts of neuroanatomy rely on sections of space, our ideas of how neurones grow come from snapshots in time. Neurones are born within the inner lining of the ventricular cavities that lie at the centre of the brain. They migrate into outer layers of neurones forming layers and nuclei – populations of cells serving a particular function. They extend fine fibres, reaching for appropriate neighbours to communicate with. One of these, the axon, contributes to information highways connecting distant regions of the brain. Finally, connections and fibres are remodelled as information itself shapes the structure of individual cells. Piecing together brain cell structure at different time-points has begun to give clues as to how cells might interact and shape themselves as they grow. However our model of brain development is still derived from glimpses of individual cells or by identifying populations by means which inevitably obscure the fine details of individual cells. Sections and snapshots remain, for the time being, the basis of our understanding of neuroanatomy."

Acknowledgements:

The process involved a rich dialogue with many scientists and institutions including:
Division of Anatomy, Cell and Human Biology, GKT School of Medical Sciences, Kings College, London. Dr Colin Stolkin. Anatomy and specimens. Dr. Alistair Hunter. Photography of specimens in the dissecting rooms. Thanks to Donald Farr, Andy, George and Kirsty.

Institute of Cognitive Neurology, London. Prof. Richard Frackowiak, Dr. Eleanor Maguire, Brain scanning, enlargement of the hippocamus in taxi drivers.

The Rockerfeller Medical Library, Institute of Neurology.

MRC Centre for Developmental Neurobiology, Kings College, London. Prof. Philip Gordon-Weeks. The living neurone, its growth and development; control of movement in growth at the growth cone of neurones. Dr. Jim Cohen. Confocal microscopy. The motor neurone, mapping towards target cells. Fabric Prin. Staining of chick neurones.

XVII World Neuroscience Conference. Cognitive neurology. London, June 2001

Wellcome Library for the History and Understanding of Medicine.

MRC Centre For Synaptic Plasticity. Dept of Anatomy, School of Medical Sciences, Bristol. Prof. Graham Collingridge. Glutamate receptors, Ca2+ signalling and plasticity in the hippocampus. Dr. Eleck Molinar. Site directed antibodies, glutamate receptors, structure and localisation. Intra cellular trafficking and synaptic targeting. Dr. Andrew Doherty. The development of drugs that will selectively activate or block two closely related neuroreceptors (the metabotropic glutamate receptors types 1 and 5 – mGlu1 & mGlu5)

Department of Anatomy, University College, London. Dr. Dave Becker. Gap junction channels; inter neurone communication. Mark Termain. Electron microscopy. Jane Pedjinky, Photography.

The Gordon Museum, Guy's Campus, Kings College, London

Richard Sotto, Presentation Technology, Kodak Ltd, Hemel Hempstead

Right and previous page:
Andrew Carnie
images from *Magic Forest*
Photos: courtesy of the artist

Katharine Dowson

Project title: Dyslexia

Title of Work/s:

Word search
Scrabble board 2001

Word play
Junior scrabble and wooden school
desk 2001

Dyslexics
Acrylic, aluminium light box 2002

You have 5 Seconds
MDF, acrylic paint 2001

Chromosome puzzle
Acrylic 2002

Historical Material:

William Healy's juvenile psychopathic test with score booklet. Wood
form board with picture cubes. 1914
Science Museum (ref. 1996–277/199)

Intelligence test. Management
Consultants Limited, form board B.
Chart and wooden blocks
Science Museum (ref. 1994–1255/23)

Drever and Collins Performance
Test of Intelligence. 1928
Science Museum (ref. 2000–856)

Project Statement:

I am using my own experience as a
dyslexic to bring out the sense of
frustration, felt particularly as a child
at school, where the emphasis is
entirely on the 3Rs (reading, writing,
and arithmetic). Intelligent children
at five years of age can see that they
are unable to read while their con-
temporaries can, and they are quick
to find fault with themselves. It is
often the early loss of confidence in
their own abilities which causes
problems later.

As a dyslexic I have been through
many IQ tests that seem to base
intelligence on your language and
numeric skills. Fewer questions are
devoted to spatial awareness and
creativity – all associated with the
right side of the brain and with
dyslexia. Therefore your weaknesses
are exposed while your strengths
are not fully analyzed.

Project Development:

In the late 1960s, dyslexia was only
recognised as a condition by a very
few educationalists. Most children
were labeled slow and never given
the chance to overcome their difficulties. I was lucky enough to be one of
the few who was identified as being
"orally deaf and visually blind", and
consequently spent the rest of my
schooling being IQ tested to prove
to the exam authorities that I was
dyslexic.

The more I researched into dyslexia
the more theories I encountered as
to the causes, from genetic causes to
those in foetal brain development,
as well as the quest for an early
diagnostic test.

I began working with Dr Piers
Cornelissen of the Neural Basis of
Reading Group, Newcastle University
Psychology Department, and
Dr Hanson, Senior Scientific Officer
for fMRI and Image Analysis for
the Oxford University MRC inter-
disciplinary Research Centre for
Cognitive Neuroscience. They are
researching into the part of the brain
which processes words and the differences there may be with the way
a dyslexic's brain functions in this
area. I had an fMRI scan as part of
this on-going research, and whilst
in the scanner I performed tests to
see my brain functioning with words.
Some of the words were invented
and others were correct. The words
flashed in front of my eyes, and I had
to press a sensor to indicate if I could
recognise them or not. My brain's
activity was meanwhile being record-
ed by the computer. This real-time
fMRI shows the location of stimuli
(in my case words) in the brain and
records an approximate activation
visual map with only a few seconds'
delay. This highlights the specific
site of stimuli in the brain.

The aim of Cornelissen and
Hanson's work is to understand how
the natural differences in visual
processing affect word recognition.
What are the fundamental relationships between position coding, (for
letter strings), the dynamics of visual
attention and visual word recognition? When and where are the
significant sources of brain activity
involved in visual word recognition,
and how is this brain activity mod-
ulated by individual variation in
sensitivity to the position of objects
and/or visual attention? This research
has the long term goal of contribut-
ing to the development of specific
methods of diagnosing and helping
those who have visual-based reading
disabilities. Dr Hanson is also collab-
orating with Prof. John Stein's Senso-
rimotor Control Lab, Physiology Lab,
Oxford. I met Prof. Stein and discussed various causes of dyslexia
(including hereditary causes) – he is
investigating the auditory and visual
processing perceptual impairments
suffered by developmental dyslexics,
and to what extent these childhood
impairments give rise to measurable
differences in adults.

The discussions I had with these
scientists reminded me of the frus-
trations of the past and I began to
explore my personal memories. The
resulting work falls into three categories: the words associated with
dyslexia, IQ tests, and my physical
dyslexic self.

Scrabble, Boggle, Hang Man, word
searches and crossword puzzles all
instill a sense of frustration and fury
at one's own inadequacies. Many
encouraging remarks such as "This
shouldn't be difficult" can be so
humiliating!

The debate around the relevance
of IQ tests rages on. They are often
only testing an individual's intelligence related to that of the test

designer. Cultural and social knowledge also played a part in the early tests which later tests tried to minimise. Often a lack of balance occurs, with questions weighted towards language skills, and over the years the tests have become less three-dimensional or tactile and more paper based. They are now generally on computers. This two-dimensional format black words on white paper is often difficult for dyslexics to read quickly, as for some the words shimmer and for others they move about. All of the tests are timed, so dyslexics loose precious intelligence-scoring seconds concentrating on reading the words. All of this fills one with panic.

There is a history of dyslexia in my family and so the question of a hereditary cause is for me not debatable. I have used my own sequenced chromosomes to make a puzzle reminiscent of the early intelligence form boards used on small children, as somewhere in there, a dyslexic gene is waiting to be discovered.

Acknowledgements:

Thanks to: Dr Piers Cornelissen, Dr Paul Hanson, Dr John Stein, Dr Gabriel Jorden

Katherine Dowson
Word Play
Courtesy of the artist

Letizia Galli

Title of Work/s:
Parking
Computer animation   2001

Historical Material:
"Therapy" table game
Science Museum (ref. E 2000.722)

The family relations test, 1957
Science Museum (ref. 2000–610)

Project Statement:
My project for *Head On* focuses on the brain and mental disorders, and on anxiety disorders in particular. One of the questions which as an artist I am particularly interested in, is: what does our society commonly accept as normal behaviour and what is considered pathological?

My visual contribution for *Head On* is a computer animation called *Parking*. The video, a loop of eight different animated sketches repeated approximately every 2 minutes, is projected onto a screen. The original idea derives from a paper by John Pittinger, an American psychiatrist who maintains that he can diagnose what kind of disorder the patients of a mental health clinic suffer, by observing the way they park their cars.

Project Development:
For over ten years my artistic work has been informed by concepts related to psychotherapy, recovery and neurology. During this project I have studied anxiety disorders in particular. I have learned a lot and exchanged views with Prof. Gray from London and with several Italian psychiatrists and psychologists.

Prof. Jeffrey Gray of the Institute of Psychiatry in London is a leading expert in the field of anxiety. His approximately 450 papers include one of the best known neuropsychological models of the obsessive-compulsive (OC) syndrome. In his model OC patients suffer from hyperactivity in the BIS (behavioral inhibition system) located in the septo-hippocampal region. The BIS monitors external and internal information. When one is in real or potential danger, this system produces anxiety, increases arousal and attention, and inhibits behaviour. Hyperactivity of the BIS consequently means that OC patients attribute danger to stimuli which are innocuous. The rituals performed by the OC patient are a means of reassuring himself that the danger has been neutralised. For panic disorder, Prof. Gray has developed a more complex anatomico-functional model in which different neuro-anatomical circuits may modulate different anxious reactions.

Anxiety together with depression is widely present in our society. We have all experienced anxiety at some point. It is an unpleasant sense of apprehension, often accompanied by symptoms such as stomach upset, headache, palpitations, and perspiration. Anxiety is an alerting signal which warns us of impeding danger and enables us to deal with the threat. Normal anxiety is crucial as it could even save our life. Anxiety becomes pathological when an individual tends to overestimate the degree of danger and harm and to underestimate their ability to cope, to the extent that they can no longer live a normal life. For example, many of us perform rituals such as checking if the door is closed before going to bed. It is different when a sufferer of obsessive-compulsive disorder washes their hands 100 times a day or checks thirty times to see if the door is closed.

There have been many neuropsychological studies over the years and these often present different views. What seems to be generally accepted is that patients with anxiety suffer from dysfunctions in the cerebral cortex. In particular an observed deficit in visuo-spatial functions indicates a dysfunction of the parietal cortex of the right hemisphere, and a memory deficit indicates a dysfunction of the temporo-limbic cortex of the right hemisphere.

Acknowledgements:
Prof J. Gray, Dr. J. Pittinger, Dr. L. Moretti, Dr. L. Pesenti, Dr. A. Cescon, Dr. F. Giommi.

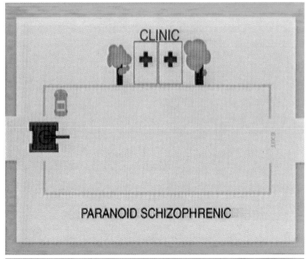

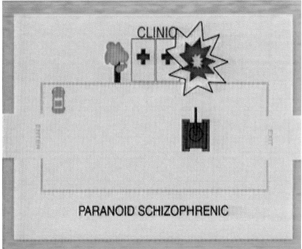

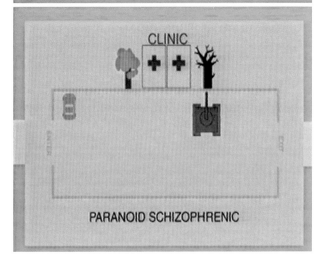

Letizia Galli
images from *Parking*
Courtesy of the artist

Claude Heath

Title of Work/s:
Head Tilting Forward
Acrylic on Linen   2001

Dust Heads
Acrylic, chalk dust and pigment
on board   2001

Stone Age Cranium
Two drawings; ink on graph paper
2000

Historical material:
Medieval image of the brain in
a manuscript written by Johann
Lindner, 1472–74
Wellcome Library (ref. Western
Ms. 55 f, fol. 93)

Benigno Bossi of Porto, Etching of
lateral view of a skull. 18th century
Wellcome (ref. anat. 337)

Piero della Francesca, *De prospectiva
pingendi*, edizione critica a cura di
Giusto Nicco Fasola, con XLIX tavole
fuori testo (Florence: G. C. Sansoni,
1942), vol. II table XXXVIII,
Description of how to draw a head
Artist's collection

Project Statement:
I have noticed that when you follow
the movement of a football across a
flat TV screen you sometimes have
the sensation that the ball is going
in a certain direction when it turns
out to have a different arc altogether
and ends up at the feet of a different
player than you had expected. The
true movements of the ball are
hidden by the flatness of the screen
until it arrives at some particular
part of the pitch. This same kind
of sensation sometimes happens
while drawing, when you attempt
to compress the sight and the touch
of a solid object onto various parts
of a flat surface.

Project Development:
Taking the idea of an experiment
or process where the outcome is not
known until completion, I have
touched the plaster cast of my
brother Toby's head with one hand
and drawn what I felt with the other
hand, the whole time working blindfolded. This allows me to translate
these sensations onto the flat surface
in a way which is not predictable.
With *Head Tilting Forward*, the original drawing was made using a multi-
coloured biro and used in a random
alternation of colours, while all the
journeys around the head started
simultaneously from one point on the
page and on the head. The marks on
the canvas represent this enlarged
drawing but only show where these
lines have crossed and where they
have changed direction, and the
resulting patterns that come from
this.

Talking over the past year to scientists who experiment with eye
movements to study the process of
perception has made me aware of
the extreme rapidity with which the
eye reaches out and takes hold of
the world, and one can see that the
patterns of these movements accu-
mulate to build up a picture of it. In
all of these works I have treated the
tactile experience of the head as if it
were visual, as in *Dust Heads*, another
blindfolded experiment with Toby's
plaster cast.

In another experiment I have used
a laser rangefinder to measure points
on a copy of a Neanderthal cranium.
This means that it is possible to
visualise the brow and crown of the
head in a number of ways as the
drawing is a projection of the process
of measurement, which has not
determined the shapes completely.

Acknowledgements:
I would like to thank the following
people for their stimulating conversation:

Dr Emily Holmes, Sub Department
of Clinical Psychology, University
College London; Professor Brian
Rogers, Department of Experimental Psychology, University of Oxford;
and Nikon UK for their support.

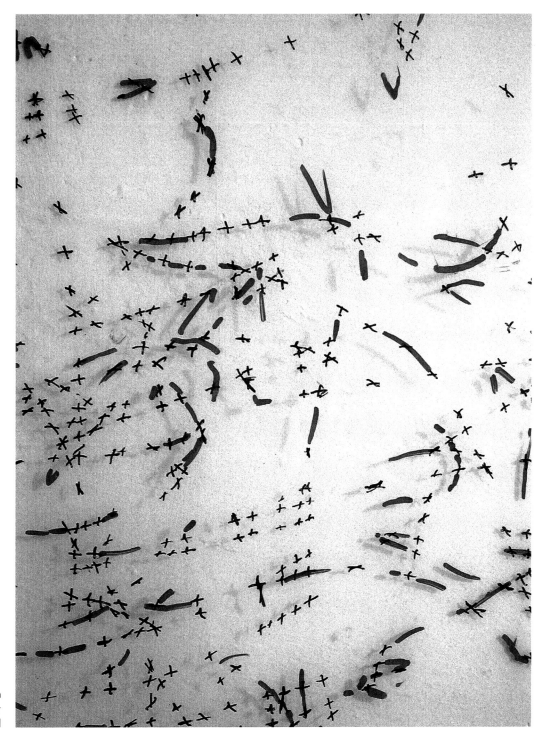

Claude Heath
Overlay drawing for
Tilting Forward, detail

Gerhard Lang

Title of Work/s:
Imago Cerebri I
Cabinet of curiosities (mixed media)
2001

Historical Material:
William Kurelek, *The Maze*
Gouache on board   1953
Bethlem Royal Hospital Archives
and Museum

William Kurelek, *Out of the Maze*
Mixed media on board   1971
Bethlem Royal Hospital Archives
and Museum

Objects in the cabinet of curiosities
include:

Freud Museum:

Egyptian stela, limestone, ca 1425
BC (ref. LDFRD 3160)
Greek statuette, ceramic, 5th–4th
cent BC (ref. LDFRD 4387)

Natural History Museum collections:

Meteorite (iron) (Mineralogy
collection)
Chalk (Mineralogy collection)
Magnetite (iodestone) (Mineralogy
collection)
Sulfur (Conil, Spain) (Mineralogy
collection)
Cinnabar (Mineralogy collection)
Three herkimer diamonds (crystals)
(Mineralogy collection)
Fluorite (green) (Mineralogy
collection)
Calcite rhombi (Mineralogy
collection)
Quartz (Mineralogy collection)
Five apatite samples (Durango,
Mexico) (Mineralogy collection)
Copper, dentritic (fern) (Mineralogy
collection)
Red organ pipe coral (Mineralogy
collection)

Small mushroom coral (Mineralogy
collection)
Small acropora (Mineralogy
collection)
Faviidae (Mineralogy collection)
Two black coral samples
(Mineralogy collection)
Two sea urchins (skeleton)
(Mineralogy collection)
Sand dollar (Mineralogy collection)
Snow owl (female) (Zoology
Collection, ref.: 1996.41.1194)
Fragment of ammonite (three pieces),
limestone (Paleontology Collection)
Almost complete ammonite
(Paleontology Collection)
Portion of a large ammonite
(Paleontology Collection)
Internal casts of ammonite
(Paleontology Collection)
Single piece of internal cast of
ammonite (Paleontology Collection)
Poplar tree, (Paleontology collection,
drawer 43C.31, No V18)
Coconut, (Paleontology Collection,
drawer 42G.25, No 21762)
Silicified conifer wood, (Paleontology
Collection, drawer 45B29 no AT
0066–10 (Araucaria)
Three cones (Paleontology Collection,
drawer 45B27)
Pasaronius brasiliensis (Psaronius),
(Paleontology Collection, drawer
35B37)
Gingo leaf, (Paleontology Collection,
drawer 41.D6, No 14838)
Coal fossil, (Paleontology Collection,
drawer 32E16, No V1867)
Tree branch fossil, (Paleontology
Collection, drawer 31D28, No 39031)

Science Museum collections:

Telescope, astrological (ref. 921–576)
Dancer binocular microscope
(ref. 1929–963)
Stereoscope by A. Claudet
(ref. 1928–870)
Dodecahedron (ref. 1876–713)
Crooke's radiometer (ref. not Inv.)
Composting stick (ref. 1878–93)
Sphygmomanometer, *c.* 1940
(ref. 1984–38/2)
Philo's thermoscope (ref. 1925–540)
Post-mortem scalpel, mid C19th
(ref. A 616958)

Private collection:

Violin and bow
Computer board
Drinking bowl, *c.* 300BC
Roman oil lamp
Etruscan bucchero
Corinthian vase
Chinese chicken (Hun Dynasty)
Abacus (Russian)
Marionette
Toy crocodile (tin)
Transformers (truck turns into
a robot)
Two molecules A) oxidon,
B) water – plastic models
Doll's house cupboard
Chess Board with figures

Project Statement:
We are representing a view of the
brain which stems from a 17th century idea: the cabinet of curiosities.
This view shows an obvious absence
of compartmentalisation, and
assumes that the brain works as
a whole, bringing together objects

and concepts from all fields of knowledge. Considered to be a creation of the universe, the cabinet of curiosities was also seen as a medium which would lead to the truth. Each added object would bring us closer to completion (truth). However, there was no way to indicate which and how many objects such a cabinet would need in order to be completed. Hence, the cabinet remained an open system. From the age of reason these cabinets became the foundation of new logical concepts which brought compartmentalisation, and the cabinets were taken apart.

In *Imago Cerebri 1* we recall the idea of the cabinet of curiosities with reference to the brain, at a time when recent advances in the neurosciences imply that we are coming close to unravelling remaining secrets of the brain. The cabinet of curiosities reminds us of some unsolved puzzles. On the one hand we can recognise all of the individual objects (natural substances, antiques, mechanics, art) and make sense of them, but on the other hand, we are faced with the question of the relationships between them. The cabinet's content with its complex meanings, relations and references remains unfathomable.

Project development:
The first two meetings with Professor Uta Frith involved exchanging ideas about our work and thoughts, and our most recent interests. We exchanged papers on our work. I was introduced to PhD students and research fellows so that I gained a deeper insight into the multifarious interests and research at the Institute of Cognitive Neuroscience at UCL. This was followed by a conversation about collaborations of two fields in general and of artists and scientists in particular. We discussed problems and weaknesses of such partnerships and their results which you could see in recent ambitious projects like *Head On*. During several meetings we gained an awareness of each other's views and, as a consequence, we established a firm foundation which, we think, is necessary, if you wish to work together successfully.

The more we talked about our work and concepts in relation to nature, the more we became aware that our contribution for *Head On* would look more like a philosophical statement about the nature of the brain and mind. The work would not show a brain, nor depict the neurological system or use scientific jargon or technology. So the title would be essential as well. At a certain point the cabinet of curiosities came into play and we were convinced that this was the route to take. In fact, ideas of that cabinet shine through in my work again and again. At the same time, Uta Frith visited the University of Uppsala, in whose collection there is a rare surviving cabinet of curiosities dating from 1632. She returned very excited about the possibilities of the idea and the images created, in particular by the juxtaposition of natural things (such as coral and stones) with manmade products (such as musical instruments and playing cards).

After I had given my talk 'The Brain is not the Landscape' at the Wellcome Trust, Professor Christopher Frith (Deputy Director of the Functional Brain Imaging Laboratory at UCL) recommended a visit to the Museum of the Bethlem Hospital. Prof. Frith made me aware of Kurelek's art work at the Hospital. When I visited the Museum, I was shown two paintings by Kurelek: A) In the Maze, B) Out of the Maze. Since I felt that these paintings showed many relations to what I had said at the Wellcome Trust, and that the show would gain substantially, we thought of showing his paintings in close vicinity to our intended work.

At that time we had already started with an intense debate via e-mail, by sending each other ideas of possible objects which could be of relevance in terms of the brain and, consequently, could become part of the cabinet which I later called *Imago Cerebri*. Simultaneously, we looked at various ways of displaying our concept, and to us the most convincing display was a circular room (diameter c. 3.5 meters and mirrored into infinity) where, from the bottom to the top, hundreds of objects would be placed in an enormous circular shelf (4.5m high). As this concept seemed to be too ambitious for *Head On*, the work was scaled down to a cupboard. To us this does not harm the concept but I decided to call the work *Imago Cerebri 1*, in order to indicate that this is the first step of a work which will lead to something more.

An important aspect of the work was the idea to bring together objects from the different collections in London. This idea challenges modern day standard requirements of conservation and compartmentalisation. Interestingly, the British Museum is planning to turn one of its huge cabinets into a room representing the collection as it looked before it was split and partially moved to the museums in Knightsbridge after 1870.

The work *Imago Cerebri 1* brings together objects from different public collections in London, private owners, and small pieces produced by me. Its contents include the personal and specific but they also reach beyond to the universal. The objects have ambiguous, multiple and sometimes contradictory meanings. This is because we interpret objects on the basis of our personal history and experience and also on the basis of our common culture. Our mind attributes meanings to the objects and tries to make sense of the relationships between them. What does the owl have to do with the computer chip; the linen with the chess board? How does the brain support these actions of the mind which combine old associations and newly formed ones?

We find ourselves confronted by the very fact that *Imago Cerebri 1* is not fathomable in logical terms. If you accept this floating nature of our concept, you can perceive more than if you started from some specifically suggested ideas. This is the moment when we start becoming fascinated.

Acknowledgements:
I would like to thank those who have loaned and helped me to get objects for the work: Professor Uta Frith, Helmut Aebischer, Lutz Becker, Edith and Hans-Fritz Lang, The Freud Museum, Sheila Halsey (Koralls, Dept. of Zoology at the NHM), Alan Hart (Department of Mineralogy at NHM), Peter Hansen (Paleontology at NHM), Dr Brys-Jones (Ornithology at NHM), Dr. Timothy Boon, Geoff Bunn and Helen Kingsley at SM, Bethlem Royal Hospital Museum and Archive, Neil Monro and Caterina Albano (curatorial assistant) for all her letters of request.

Gerhard Lang *Imago Cerebri I* Installation shots

Tim O'Riley

Title of Work/s:

Mirror
Two plywood stereoscopes,
pictographic prints mounted on
plexiglass   2001

Historical Material:

Portable stereoscope (with original
drawing by Charles Wheatstone)
and box, c. 1850
Science Museum, ref. 1884–7

Charles Wheatstone, Stereoscopic
drawings on paper (2 pairs, 2 singles),
c. 1850
Science Museum, ref. 1884–17

Stereoscopic image No. 10, Cranial
Cerebral Topography (from *The
Edinburgh stereoscopic atlas of anatomy*,
edited by David Waterstone,
Edinburgh: T.C. & E.C. Jack,
1905–1906)
Wellcome Library, ref. icv 49466

Arthur Thomson, *The anatomy of
the human eye as illustrated by enlarged
stereoscopic photographs* (Oxford:
Clarendon Press, 1912)

plate 9: Antero-posterior section of
an eye in which the anterior surface
of the iris has become closely adher-
ent to the internal surface of the
cornea

plate 22: Anterior view of the iris
(seen in isolation from the rest of
the eye)

plate 41: Interior of anterior half of
the globe of the eye (seen from front)

plate 48: Lens seen from front

plate 53: Anterior view of half of lens

plate 66: Scleral surface of portion of
ciliary body

Wellcome Library, ref. Med. XWW

Project Statement:

In *The Man who mistook his wife
for a hat*, Oliver Sacks questions
Wittgenstein's idea that the body is
the start and basis of certainty about
the world[1]. What if the body's condition or disposition somehow alters
this certainty, what if things are
presented to it that manipulate,
override or undermine its usual
perceptual mechanisms so that
certainty is replaced with doubt?

In everyday life, we are constantly
inferring whole things from fragments, interpreting and making
sense – perceptually, emotionally,
physically – of the apparent random-
ness and disorder around us. Shared
experiences enable us to make sure
that our consciousness corresponds
to the outside world. We may agree
that this table is here and that it is
green, for example. By agreeing to
what is common to a thing, the
thing becomes concrete or actual.

Illusions upset this sense of certainty. Their location in relation to
us is ambiguous and our response to
them is self-generated. With stereoscopic pictures, for example, we
know that we are looking at two flat
images yet they appear solid and
three-dimensional like things in
reality. This sense of solidity occurs
somewhere in our brain and is not
present in the pictures unless they
are seen through a stereoscope or
through special glasses. These kinds
of pictures are intriguing because
they raise a question about where
the illusion is in relation to us when
we look at it. Is it a property of the
physical image or of our eyes and
brain, or does it exist somewhere
else, being both actual and mental
simultaneously? More to the point,
doesn't everything we perceive occupy
this mysterious territory? Is the
world we see in some a sense a
product of the constant interchange
between our own internal reality
and the external, physical world?

Charles Wheatstone developed the
stereoscope in the early to mid-1830s
as a tool for analysing binocular
vision. It is a device where two
images, drawings or photographs,
which have been taken from slightly
different positions, are viewed
together and give an impression of
depth and solidity as in ordinary
human vision. The striking thing
about Wheatstone's stereoscope is
that while the two images are posi-
tioned either side of one's head, the
illusion is naturally seen as in front.
It demonstrates the remarkable
plasticity and malleability of vision
and suggests that seeing is as much
to do with projecting what we think
we see onto the world we actually see.

Wheatstone's early stereoscopic
pictures were made just prior to the
invention of photography and were
hand-drawn images of simple, often
rectilinear objects that were straight-
forward to draw from two different
points-of-view. Although the advent
of photography meant that more
complex stereoscopic pictures could
be made easily and successfully using
the camera, these early drawings have
a precision and delicacy that makes
them particularly effective when seen
through the stereoscope. Photography suggested other uses for the
technique and in the archives of the
Wellcome Trust, there are some
interesting stereo anatomical images
of the brain and eye dating from the
early 1900s that were designed as
educational tools. It is disconcerting
to look at these images in full 3D
with one's own eyes and brain.

Tim O'Riley *Mirror* Plywood stereoscope pictographic prints, mounted on plexiglass 2001

They evoke an odd sense of peering through someone else's eyes or looking into someone else's mind.

The specific brain conditions that have intrigued and unsettled me in relation to this project are not necessarily linked to stereo pictures or binocular vision, but rather question the sense of certainty that we assume when we look at things, or when we try to remember or imagine them. After contact with Professor Kennard and Professor Chris Frith, I became interested in reports of hallucinations or conditions such as visual neglect, the loss of a sense of things on one side of the visual field often associated with damage to the brain following a stroke. A striking description of visual neglect recounted a test where two patients were asked to recall the two long sides of the Piazza del Duomo, the principal square in Milan. They were asked to imagine in one case that they were facing the Duomo and in the other that they had turned their back to it.[2] From both imagined viewpoints, they omitted to mention the buildings placed on their left, so that those recalled on one occasion were neglected immediately afterwards, and vice versa. Both their perceptual and mental scanning processes seemed to omit one half of the visual field, despite the fact that their brains had somehow noted the different sides of the square.

Chris Frith explained that experiments using brain scans have shown that where visual neglect occurs, the brain is actually registering a stimulus without the subject being aware of seeing anything. Similarly, scans indicate that the brain registers differences in the stimulus even though the subject may not recognise or perceive those differences. Hallucination is the opposite in the sense that a thing is perceived without any stimulus input. Chris also showed me one demonstration that highlights what is called change blindness: two pictures are projected in rapid succession and the viewer is asked to note anything unusual about what they are seeing. The first image showed an aeroplane, and in the other, the same aeroplane with one of its engines missing. This difference was not apparent for quite some time even though in reality my brain would have been registering the difference. That is, what I thought was in front of me and what was actually in front of me did not immediately coincide. The question seems to be: how does the brain distinguish activity associated with expecting and imagining, from activity associated with actually seeing?

For many years, vision was regarded as a passive process, often likened to the workings of a camera obscura (literally a dark room) whereby an image of the outside world was projected onto a screen and so made visible to the onlooker within. Modern thinking, however, seems to suggest that vision is an active process in which the brain constructs the sense of what is seen, and at an extreme level, so contributes to the very nature of the thing seen. As the neurologist Leif Finkel says, the picture of the world that we see does not exist as a single, complete representation somewhere in the brain. It is an emergent property of the system. He goes on: "We inhabit a mixed realm of sensation and interpretation, and the boundary between them is never openly revealed to us. And amid this tenuous situation, our cortex makes up little stories about the world, and softly hums them to us to keep us from getting scared at night.[3]"

Acknowledgements:

I would like to acknowledge: Robin Clifton; Professor Chris Frith and Professor Christopher Kennard; Chelsea College of Art & Design; Eye Animation Studios, London.

1
Oliver Sacks, *The man who mistook his wife for a hat*, London: Picador 1986, p43.

2
E. Bisiach and C. Luzzatti, "Unilateral neglect of Representational Space", *Cortex*, 1978, 14: pp129–133, described in E. de Renzi, *Disorders of Space Exploration and Cognition*, Chichester: Wiley 1982, p.110. A similar case is referred to in Oliver Sacks, *The man who mistook his wife for a hat*, p14).

3
L.H. Finkel, The Construction of Perception, *Zone (Incorporations)*, 1992, 6: pp395–405, p404.

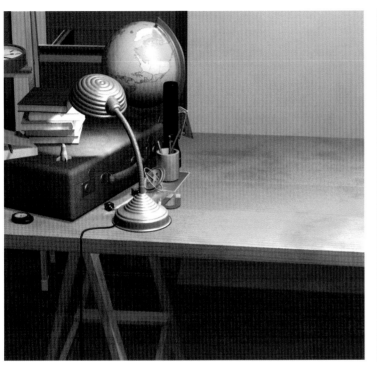 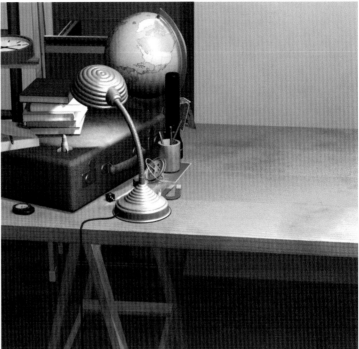

Tim O'Riley *Mirror* Pictographic prints
Image courtesy of the artist

List of Works (by artists)

J. F. Gautier d'Agoty
Muscles of the eye and larynx and the head shown with a section of the skull removed
Muscles of the right side of the head and neck
Subcutaneous blood vessels of the head and neck
Colour mezzotints by J.F. d'Agoty after himself, 1745–48
(Paris: Sieur Gautier)
Wellcome Library, refs. 33491i, 33381i, 498088i
p. 10

Félix Vicq d'Azyr
Traité d'anatomie de physiologie avec des planches coloriées représentant au naturel les divers organes de l'homme et des animaux
Paris: de l'imprimerie de François Amb. Didot l'Aîné
1786, plate 19
Engraving illustrating dissection of the arterial system at the base of the brain
Wellcome Library
ref. EPB F. 694

Osi Audu
Conscious and Unconscious Mind
Steel and yellow rope
2002

Outer and Inner Head
Acrylic and wool on canvas (diptych)
2002
p. 37

The Seeing Mind
Steel, rope, animatronic eye and perspex
2002
p. 34

William Bally
Wooden box containing 60 small phrenological heads
c.1831
Science Museum
ref. A642804

John Beard
Self portrait Head 10
Oil on wax on canvas
2000
Stephen Lacey Gallery

Self portrait Head 11
Oil and wax on canvas
1996–2000
Stephen Lacey Gallery

Charles Bell
The Anatomy of the Brain Explained in a Series of Plates, 1823
Watercolour illustration from a manuscript copy of Bell's work, plate I
Sections of the brain
Wellcome Library
ref. Western Ms.1121
p. 9

Tony Bevan
Head PC008
Acrylic on canvas
2000
Michael Hue-Williams Fine Art Gallery
p. 17

Govert Bidloo
Anatomia humani corporis, centum & quinque tabulis, per artificiosissis. G. de Lairesse ad vivum delineatis...
Amsterdam: sumptibus viduae Joannis à Someren, 1685, plate VII
Dissection of the brain: the dura mater
Wellcome Library
ref. EPB F. 2051

Benigno Bossi of Porto
Etching of lateral view of a skull
18th century
Wellcome Library
ref. anat. 337

Ian Breakwell
In the wings
Photo-diptych, 1993
Anthony Reynolds Gallery
p. 15

Paul Broca
Cast of the top section of the skull of 'Jenny', aged 15
Phrenological areas marked with different colours and numbers, 1876
Hunterian Museum
Royal College of Surgeons
ref. RCSHM/D714

Broca goniometer
Equipment for measuring the facial angle and facial triangle
French, 1862–1900
Science Museum
ref.1980-1101

Santiago Ramón y Cajal
Neuronismo o reticularismo? Las pruebas objetivas de la unidad anatómica de la celulas nerviosas
Madrid: Archivos de neurobiología
v.13, 1933
Figs 157–158, 159–160. Neurones
Wellcome Library
ref. Med. XWL

Santiago Ramón y Cajal
Recuerdos de mi vida
Madrid: Impr. de J. Pueyo, 1923
Fig. 4a–5a
Neurones
Wellcome Library
ref. Med. Hist2 BZP(Ramon)

Petrus Camper
Dissertation physique sur les différence réelles que présentent les traits chez les hommes de différents pays et de différents âges... Utrecht: chez B. Wild et J. Altheer, 1791, plate III Facial differentiations
Wellcome Library
ref. EPB MLS/C/ CAM

Andrew Carnie
Magic Forest: slide dissolve work
Two projectors, time dissolve unit, 160 slides, three gauze screens, aluminium supporting bars, two plinths, 2001
Sponsored by Kodak, Arts and Humanities Research Board, and The Faculty of Arts Southampton University
Front and back cover and pp. 24, 43, 45

Heidi Cartwright
Brain falling apart
Manipulated photograph of the superior aspect of a human brain
Wellcome Photo Library

Retro brain
Digital image of the human brain in symmetrical tiles
Wellcome Photo Library

Coloured image of the anterior aspect of the human brain
Wellcome Photo Library
p. 11

Annie Cattrell
Seeing
Resin encapsulated in hot cure resin
2001
p. 22

Hearing
Resin encapsulated in hot cure resin
2001
p. 23

Riccardo de Sanctis
Imaging the brain; envisioning the mind
A short film about scientific investigations of the brain, 2002

René Descartes
L'Homme et un traitté de la formation du foetus
Paris: chez Charles Angot, 1664, p.81
Illustration of the co-ordination of the sense organs and the brain
Wellcome Library
ref. EPB 20200/B

Katharine Dowson
Word search
Scrabble board
2001

Word play
Junior scrabble and wooden school desk
2001
p. 45

Dyslexics
Acrylic, aluminium light box
2002
p. 27

You have 5 Seconds
MDF, acrylic paint
2001

Chromosome puzzle
Acrylic
2002

Robert Fludd
Tomus secundus. De supernaturali, naturali, praeternaturali et contranaturali microcosmi historia
Oppenhemij: impensis Johannis Theodori de Bry, 1619
Tractatus I, sectio II, portio III, p.47
Frontispiece of *De animae memorativae scientia, quae vulgo ars memoriae vocatur*
'Ars memoriae'
'The Art of Memory'
The eye of imagination and the five mental memory 'loci'
Wellcome Library
ref. EPB 2326/D

Piero della Francesca
De prospectiva pingendi
edizione critica a cura di Giusto Nicco Fasola, con XLIX tavole fuori testo
Florence: G. C. Sansoni, 1942, vol. II
table XXXVIII
Description of how to draw a head
Artist's collection

Elizabeth Frink
Desert Quartet I
Bronze, edition of 6, 1989
Beaux Arts
p. 14

Letizia Galli
Parking
Computer animation
2001
p. 47

Claude Heath
Head Tilting Forward
Acrylic on linen
2001
p.30

Dust Heads
Acrylic, chalk dust and pigment on board
2001

Stone Age Cranium
Two drawings
Ink on graph paper
2000

David Hockney
Portrait of Brad Bontems
Pencil and gouache on white paper using a mirror lens
2000
p. 6

Patrick Hughes
Perfectspective
Oil on board
2001
Angela Flowers Gallery

Athanasius Kircher
Arca Noë, in tres libros digesta
Amsterdam: apud Joannem Janssonium a Waesberge
1675, p.117
'Noah's Ark'
Wellcome Library
ref. EPB 31211/D

Jan Amos Komensky
Orbis sensualium pictus, hoc est, omnium principalium in mundo rerum, et in vita actionum, pictura et nomenclatura...
Translated into English by Charles Hoole 11 ed., London: printed and sold by John and Benj. Sprint, 1728, pp. 4–5
'The Living Alphabet'
Wellcome Library
ref. EPB 18500/A

William Kurelek
The Maze
Gouache on board
1953
Bethlem Royal Hospital Archives and Museum

Out of the Maze
Mixed media on board
1971
Bethlem Royal Hospital Archives and Museum

William Healy
Juvenile psychopathic test with score booklet
Wood form board with picture cubes, 1914
Science Museum
ref. 1996-277/199

Johann Host von Romberch Kyrspensis
Congestorium Artificiose Memorie
Venice: in edibus Georgii de Rusconibus
1520, sig. e.vi.v.–e.vii.r
'The Living Alphabet'
Wellcome Library
ref. EPB 5542/A

Gerhard Lang
Imago Cerebri I
Cabinet of curiosities
Mixed media
2001
pp. 51, 53

George E. Madeley
Authored by Cornelius Donovan.
Phrenological chart with portraits of historical figures and illustrations of skulls exhibiting racial characteristics
Lithograph, London: H. Renshaw
c.1850
Wellcome Library, ref. 27927i

after G. Spratt
A physiognomist whose body is made up of faces, sitting at a table diagnosing people's physiognomic characteristics with the help of a book
Coloured lithograph, 1831
Wellcome Library
ref. 35150i
p. 8

Mark G Pick D.C., F.I.C.S.
The circuitry within
Latex and fibre optic model of the brain, spinal cord and peripheral nerves, cast from a human cadaver

Tim O'Riley
Mirror
Two plywood stereoscopes, pictographic prints mounted on plexiglass
2001
pp. 55, 57

Frederik Ruysch
Epistola anatomica, problematica nona. Authore Andrea Ottomaro Goelicke... De cursu arteriarum per piam matrem cerebrum involventem, Opera Omnia, vol. I
Amsterdam: apud Jansonio-Waesbergios, 1744, plate X
Wax injection of the blood vessels in the arachnoid and pia mater
Wellcome Library
ref. EPB/MSL/C/RUY

Johann Jakob Scheuchzer
Physique sacrée
Amsterdam: chez Pierre Schenk and Pierre Morties, 1732–37, vol.VII
plate DXCIII
Brain and spinal cord
Illustration from Eustachio interpreting the *funis argenteus* in *Ecclesiastes*
Wellcome Library
ref. EBP/D 46988/D

Arthur Thomson
The anatomy of the human eye as illustrated by enlarged stereoscopic photographs
Oxford: Clarendon Press, 1912
Wellcome Library
ref. Med. XWW

Joseph Towne
Wax model of an un-dissected brain
1860–70s
Gordon Museum

Wax model of a dissected brain of a baby (whole)
1860–70s
Gordon Museum

Wax model of a dissected brain of a baby, cut hemispherically
1860–70s
Gordon Museum

Wax model of a magnified brain with section of the eye
1860–70s
Gordon Museum

Wax model of a dissection of the head and neck
1860–70s
Gordon Museum

Wax model of a dissection of a brain
1860–70s
Hunterian Museum
Royal College of Surgeons
ref. S 208
p. 12

Richard Wentworth
Twenty seven minutes, twenty two nouns, seven adjectives
Book, assorted materials on mirror glass, 1999
Lisson Gallery
p. 13

Charles Wheatstone
Portable stereoscope with original drawing and box, c.1850
Science Museum
ref. 1884-7

Stereoscopic drawings on paper
2 pairs, 2 singles, c.1850
Science Museum
ref. 1884-17

Thomas Willis
The anatomy of the brain in Dr Willis's Practice of physick, being the whole works of that renowned and famous physician
London: printed for T. Dring, C Harper and J. Leigh, 1684
Fig.I and II
Brain and Brain section
Wellcome Library
ref. EPB/C/WIL

G. Wingendorp
Frontispiece to catalogue of Ole Worm's museum catalogue
Museum Wormianum
Line engraving, 1655
Wellcome Library
ref. icv. 19345

Pat York
Neural Nexus 2/5
imbue print
2001
p.16

List of Works (by object)

Angiogram x-ray. Lateral view of the skull, showing a brain tumour
Wellcome Library
ref. No019206Coo

Anterior horn neuron
Wellcome Photo Library
ref. Noo13853

Blood-flow maps of the brain for age-matched Alzheimer's dementia, and normal patients
Wellcome Photo Library
ref. Noo16670Coo

Brain toys and souvenirs
Various materials
1960s–present

Charles Babbage's left cerebral hemisphere (half his brain), labelled 'Homo'
Hunterian Museum
Royal College of Surgeons
ref. RCSHM/D 685
part 2
p. 5

Colour-enhanced CT scan of the brain in a stroke patient
Wellcome Photo Library
No Noo13781C

Computer generated image of the brain – from above
Wellcome Photo Library
ref. Noo13851C

Digitised MRI scan of the head
Wellcome Photo Library
ref. Noo13862C

Drever and Collins Performance Test of Intelligence, 1928
Science Museum
ref. 2000-856

'Exploded' skull in glass case by Émile Deyrolle fils
Paris, France, Early 20th century
Hunterian Museum
Royal College of Surgeons
ref. RCSHMZ/ 53

The family relations test, 1957
Science Museum
ref. 2000-610

Horizontal section through occipital region of the cerebral hemisphere of an adult Egyptian
Presented by Professor Elliot Smith, 1904
Hunterian Museum
Royal College of Surgeons
ref. RCSHM/D 728d

The human brain, divided according to Bernard Hollander's system of phrenology
Photomechanical reproduction with pen and ink rendering, c.1902
Wellcome Library
ref. 27959i

Intelligence test
Management Consultants Limited
Form board B
Chart and wooden blocks
Science Museum
ref. 1994-1255/23

Lithograph of the death mask of Martin, a parricide (from the working archive of the phrenologist Bernard Hollander), c.1835
Wellcome Library
ref.28231i
p. 9

Longitudinal section of a human foetus at 10–12 week gestation
Wellcome Photo Library
ref. No Noo13312C

Medieval image of the brain in a manuscript written by Johann Lindner, 1472–74
Wellcome Library
ref. Western Ms. 55 f, fol. 93

Ntutu Agwu group effigy, with back to back figures of a male and female (with child in her arms)
Carved wood, 1870–1930
Ibo people
Southern Nigeria
Science Museum
ref. A 657365

Porcelain phrenological bust on a plinth, c.1825
Science Museum
ref. A642806

'Therapy' table game
Science Museum
Ref. E 2000.722

Three perspectives of a skull sectioned and labelled according to an unorthodox system of phrenology Pen drawing, 19th century
Wellcome Library
ref. 27670i

Small carved kneeling female figure with five infants
Hardwood, mirror and glass
Possibly Bakongo people
Congo, 1850–1920
Science Museum
ref. A652609

Stereoscopic image No. 10
Cranial Cerebral Topography
from The Edinburgh stereoscopic atlas of anatomy
Edited by David Waterstone,
Edinburgh: T.C. & E.C. Jack, 1905–1906
Wellcome Library
ref. icv 49466
p. 33

Wooden chair, stained black
Congo, n.d.
Science Museum
ref. A 602179

Head on

art with the brain in mind

A Wellcome Trust Exhibition
at the Science Museum, London
15 March – 28 July 2002

For Lukas and Jackson, Juliette and Marcel, and their beautiful minds.

Exhibition

Exhibition produced by the Wellcome Trust

Curated by Caterina Albano, Ken Arnold and Marina Wallace

Science Museum Team: Mikhail Baraclough, Tim Boon, Geoff Bunn, Peter Davison, Andrew Nahum, Ann Newmark, Helen Kingsley, and Tim Molloy

Additional scientific input from The European Dana Alliance for the Brain

Designed by David Bentheim & Co

Kodak

Andrew Carnie work has been sponsored by Kodak

Catalogue

First published in March 2002

by Artakt Ltd.
www.artakt.co.uk

Compiled with the assistance of The Wellcome Trust

Designed by: Herman Lelie
Typesetting by: Stefania Bonelli
Printed by: PJ Print, London

All photographs are by Luciano Sansone, unless otherwise credited

Cover: Andrew Carnie *Magic Forest* Photo by Luciano Sansone

ISBN: 0-9542416-0-6

Exhibitions are collaborative projects. *Head on* has been made possible with help from many people and organisations, including:

3D Systems, Helmut Aebischer, Patricia Allderidge, Elizabeth Allen, Angela Flowers Gallery, Anthony Reynolds Gallery, Bergit Arends, Jackson Arnold, Richard Aspin, Ann Attwood, Osi Audu, Mikhail Baraclough, John Beard, Beaux Arts, Dave Becker, Lutz Becker, David Bentheim, Bethlem Royal Hospital Archives and Museum, Tony Bevan, Tony Bish, Colin Blain, Colin Blakemore, Eleanor Boddington, Stefania Bonelli, Tim Boon, Ian Breakwell, Geoff Bunn, Andrew Carnie, Annie Cattrell, Simon Chaplin, A. Cescon, Robin Clifton, Jim Cohen, Chelsea College of Art & Design, Graham Collingridge, Robin Cole-Hamilton, Piers Cornelissen, Erica Davies, Peter Davison, Miriam de Lacy, Riccardo de Sanctis, Andrew Doherty, Ray Dolan, Katharine Dowson, Bill Edwards, Paul Ensom, Eye Animation Studios, Richard Frackowiak, Freud Museum, Chris Frith, Uta Frith, Letizia Galli, F. Giommi, Gordon Museum, Philip Gordon-Weeks, David Graves, Jeffrey Gray, Susan Greenfield, Richard Gregory, Claire Griffiths, Sheila Halsey, Lukas Hamilton, Paul Hanson, Alan Hart, Claude Heath, Hobarts Ltd., David Hockney, Emily Holmes, Patrick Hughes, Alistair Hunter, Hunterian Museum, The Royal College of Surgeons of England, Anya Hurlbert, Roland Jackson, Denna Jones, Gabriel Jorden, Brian Kane, Martin Kemp, Christopher Kennard, Helen Kingsley, Kodak, Edith and Hans-Fritz Lang, Gerhard Lang, Beverley Laing, Herman Lelie, Lisson Gallery, Mark Lythgoe, Eleanor Maguire, Ian & Laura Marsh, Xerxes Mazda, Michael Hue-Williams Fine Art Gallery, Eleck Molinar, Tim Molloy, Neil Monro, L. Moretti, Andrew Nahum, Natural History Museum, Anne Newark, Nikon UK, Danielle Olsen, Tim O'Riley, Claire Partington, Jane Pedjinky, L. Pesenti, Marc Pick, Robert Prys-Jones, Jane Quinn, Marc Quinn, Rockfeller Medical Library, Institute of Neurology, Brian Rogers, Steven Rose, Saatchi Gallery, Luciano Sansone, William Schupbach, Tim Shallice, Nasira Sheik-Miller, Laurence Smaje, Elaine Snell, Steve Smith, John Stein, Steven Lacey Gallery, Colin Stolkin, Doron Swade, John Symons, Mark Termain, Diego Trolliet, Wallace/Kemp Artakt staff, Sarah Wang, The Wellcome Trust Library for the History and Understanding of Medicine staff, Juliette, Marcel and Paul Wallace, Richard Wentworth, Richard Whingate, Jenny Whiting, Neil Williams, Bob Wybourn, Pat York